DK EYEWITNESS TRAVEL

15-MINUTE
GERMAN

DK EYEWITNESS TRAVEL

15-MINUTE
GERMAN

LEARN GERMAN
IN JUST 15
MINUTES A DAY

SYLVIA GOULDING

London, New York, Munich, Melbourne,
and Delhi

Dorling Kindersley Limited
Senior Editor Angeles Gavira
Project Art Editor Vanessa Marr
DTP Designer John Goldsmid
Production Controller Luca Frassinetti
Publishing Manager Liz Wheeler
Managing Art Editor Philip Ormerod
Publishing Director Jonathan Metcalf
Art Director Bryn Walls

Language content for Dorling Kindersley by
g-and-w publishing

Produced for Dorling Kindersley by
Schermuly Design Co.
Art Editor Hugh Schermuly
Project Editor Cathy Meeus
Special photography Mike Good

First American Edition, 2005

Published in the United States by
DK Publishing, Inc., 375 Hudson Street,
New York, New York 10014

05 06 07 08 09   10 9 8 7 6 5 4 3 2 1

A Cataloging-in-Publication record for this book
is available from the Library of Congress.

ISBN 0-7566-0923-2

15-Minute German is also available in a pack
with two CDs (ISBN 0-7566-0930-5)

Color reproduction by Colourscan, Singapore
Printed and bound in China by Leo Paper
Products Limited

Discover more at
www.dk.com

Contents

How to use this book

This main part of the book is devoted to 12 themed chapters, broken down into five 15-minute daily lessons, the last of which is a revision lesson. So, in just 12 weeks you will have completed the course. A concluding reference section contains a menu guide and English-to-German and German-to-English dictionaries.

Warm up and clock

Each day starts with a one-minute warm-up that encourages you to recall vocabulary or phrases you have learned previously. A clock to the right of the heading bar indicates the amount of time you are expected to spend on each exercise.

Instructions

Each exercise is numbered and introduced by instructions that explain what to do. In some cases additional information is given about the language point being covered.

Cultural/Conversational tip

These panels provide additional insights into life in Germany and language usage.

Text styles

Distinctive text styles differentiate German and English, and the pronunciation guide (see right).

In conversation

Illustrated dialogues reflecting how vocabulary and phrases are used in everyday situations appear throughout the book.

How to use the flap

The book's cover flaps allow you to conceal the German so that you can test whether you have remembered correctly.

Revision pages

A recap of selected elements of previous lessons helps to reinforce your knowledge.

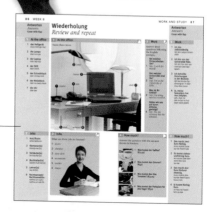

Useful phrases
Selected phrases relevant to the topic help you speak and understand.

EATING AND DRINKING 19

Pronunciation guide

Many German sounds will already be familiar to you, but a few require special attention. Take note of how these letters are pronounced:

ch	pronounced from the back of the throat, as in the Scottish *loch*
j	pronounced *y* as in *yes*
r	rolled, produced from the back of the throat
s	pronounced either *s* as in *see* or *z* as in *zoo*
sch	pronounced *sh* as in *ship*
ß	a special character that represents a double *ss*
v	pronounced *f* as in *foot*
w	pronounced *v* as in *van*
z/tz	pronounced *ts* as in *pets*

German vowels can be tricky, with the same vowel having a number of different pronunciations. Watch out also for these combinations that may look like familiar English sounds, but are pronounced differently in German:

au	as the English *now*
ee	as the English *lay*
ei	as the English *high*
eu	as the English *boy*
ie	as the English *see*

After each word or phrase you will find a pronunciation transcription. Read this, bearing in mind the tips above, and you will achieve a comprehensible result. But remember that the transcription can only ever be an approximation and that there is no real substitute for listening to and mimicking native speakers.

Say it
In these exercises you are asked to apply what you have learned using different vocabulary.

5 Say it

Do you have a single room, please?

For six nights.

Is breakfast included?

Dictionary
A mini-dictionary provides ready reference from English to German and German to English for 2,500 words.

Menu guide
Use this guide as a reference for food terminology and popular German dishes.

132 DICTIONARY

Dictionary
English to German

128 MENU GUIDE

Menu guide

1 Warm up

The Warm Up panel appears at the beginning of each topic. Use it to reinforce what you have already learned and to prepare yourself for moving ahead with the new subject.

Guten Tag
Hello

In formal situations, Germans greet each other with a handshake. They are addressed with title—**Herr** (for men) and **Frau** (for women)—and last name. Nowadays the title **Fräulein** (*Miss*) is rarely used for adult women. Young people may greet each other with a kiss on each cheek.

Hallo!
Hal-loe
Hello!

2 Words to remember

Learn these expressions. Conceal the German with the cover flap and test yourself.

Guten Tag. goo-ten tahk	*Hello/Good day.*
Guten Abend/Nacht. goo-ten ah-bent /nukht	*Good evening/night.*
Bis bald/morgen. biss balt/mor-gen	*See you soon/tomorrow.*
Auf Wiedersehen/ Tschüss. owf vee-der-zay- en/tchews	*Goodbye. (formal/informal)*

> ■ **Cultural tip** In addition to proper names, all nouns start with a capital letter in German—for example, "der Tag" (the day), as in "Guten Tag" (good day).

3 In conversation: formal

Guten Tag. Ich heiße Martina Li.
goo-ten tahk. ikh high-se mar-teen-a lee

Hello. My name is Martina Li.

Guten Tag. Michael Brand, freut mich.
goo-ten tahk. mikh-ah-ail brant, froyt mikh

Hello. Michael Brand, pleased to meet you.

Freut mich.
froyt mikh

Pleased to meet you.

4 Put into practice

Join in this conversation. Read the German beside the pictures on the left and then follow the instructions to make your reply. Then test yourself by concealing the answers with the cover flap.

Guten Abend, Herr Gohl.
goo-ten ah-bent, hair goel
Good evening, Mr. Gohl.

Say: Good evening.

Guten Abend.
goo-ten ah-bent

Ich heiße Ilse Gerlach.
ikh high-se ilze gair-lakh.
My name is Ilse Gerlach.

Say: Pleased to meet you.

Freut mich.
froyt mikh

5 Useful phrases

Familiarize yourself with these words. Read them aloud several times and try to memorize them. Conceal the German with the cover flap and test yourself.

What's your name?	**Wie heißen Sie?** vee high-sen zee
My name is Thomas.	**Ich heiße Thomas.** ikh high-se toe-mass
Pleased to meet you.	**Freut mich.** froyt mikh
Thank you.	**Danke.** dun-ke

6 In conversation: informal

Also, bis morgen?
ull-zoe, biss mor-gen

So, see you tomorrow?

Ja, auf Wiedersehen.
yah, owf vee-der-zay-en

Yes, goodbye.

Tschüss. Bis bald.
tchews. biss balt

Goodbye. See you soon.

Say "hello" and "goodbye" in German. (pp.8–9)

Now say "My name is…". (pp.8–9)

Say "Mr" and "Mrs". (pp.8–9)

Die Verwandten
Relatives

In German things are masculine, feminine, or neuter, taking a different form of "the" according to gender: **der** (masculine), **die** (feminine), and **das** (neuter). There is no easy way of knowing the gender of a word; you will have to memorize them individually.

2 Match and repeat

Look at the numbered family members in this scene and match them with the vocabulary list at the side. Read the German words aloud. Now, conceal the list with the cover flap and test yourself.

1 **der Großvater**
dair groes-fah-ter

2 **der Bruder**
dair broo-der

3 **die Schwester**
dee shvess-ter

4 **der Vater**
dair fah-ter

5 **die Mutter**
dee moot-ter

6 **die Großmutter**
dee groes-moot-ter

7 **der Sohn**
dair zoen

8 **die Tochter**
dee tokh-ter

❶ *grandfather*   ❸ *sister*
brother ❷   ❹ *father*
❺ *mother*

grandmother ❻ ❼ *son*   ❽ *daughter*

Conversational tip In German the word "ein" (a/an) changes according to the gender of the noun—for example, "Ich habe eine Schwester" (I have a sister), but "Ich habe einen Sohn" (I have a son).

3 Words to remember: relatives

Germans commonly refer to their spouses as **mein Mann** (*my man*) or **meine Frau** (*my woman*). This is not impolite, but a shortened version of **mein Ehemann** and **meine Ehefrau**.

der Ehemann	**die Ehefrau**
dair	dee
ay-amunn	ay-afrow
husband	*wife*

Ich bin verheiratet.
ikh bin fer-hye-rah-tet
I'm married.

children	**die Kinder** dee kin-der
brother-in-law/ sister-in-law	**der Schwager/die Schwägerin** dair shvar-ger/dee shvay-ge-rin
half-brother/half-sister	**der Halbbruder/die Halbschwester** dair hulp-broo-der/dee hulp-shvess-ter
stepson/stepdaughter	**der Stiefsohn/die Stieftochter** dair shteef-zohn/dee shteef-tokh-ter
stepfather/stepmother	**der Stiefvater/die Stiefmutter** dair shteef-fah-ter/dee shteef-moot-ter
I have two sons	**Ich habe zwei Söhne.** ikh hah-be tsvie zer-ne.

4 Words to remember: numbers

Memorize these words and then test yourself using the cover flap.

In German the plural is formed by adding an "en," "e," "er," or "s" to the end of the word, as in **Frau/Frauen** (*woman/women*), **Tag/Tage** (*day/days*), **Mann/Männer** (*man/men*), **Auto/Autos** (*car/cars*). In many cases the main vowel changes to an umlaut, as in **der Bruder/die Brüder** (*brother/brothers*). In others there is no change.

one	**eins** ients
two	**zwei** tsvie
three	**drei** drie
four	**vier** feer
five	**fünf** fewnf
six	**sechs** zeks
seven	**sieben** zee-ben
eight	**acht** akht
nine	**neun** noyn
ten	**zehn** tsayn

5 Say it

One sister.

Three sons.

Two brothers.

Meine Familie
My family

1 Warm up

Say the German for as many members of the family as you can. (pp.10–11)

Say "I have two sons." (pp.10–11)

There are two ways of saying "you" in German: **Sie** for people you have just met or don't know very well, and **du** for family and friends. There are also different words for "your" (see below). It is best to use **Sie** when you first meet someone and wait until he or she invites you to use **du**.

2 Words to remember

The words for "my" and "your" change, depending on the gender and number of the word to which they relate.

mein mine	*my (with masculine or neuter)*
meine mye-ne	*my (with feminine)*
meine mye-ne	*my (with plural)*
dein dine	*your (informal, with masculine or neuter)*
deine dye-ne	*your (informal, with feminine)*
deine dye-ne	*your (informal, with plural)*
Ihr eer	*your (formal, with masculine or neuter)*
Ihre ee-re	*your (formal, with feminine or plural)*

Das sind meine Eltern.
duss zint mye-ne
ell-tern
These are my parents.

3 In conversation

Haben Sie Kinder?
hah-ben zee kin-der

Do you have any children?

Ja, ich habe zwei Töchter.
yah, ikh hah-be tsvie terkh-ter

Yes, I have two daughters.

Hier sind meine Töchter. Und Sie?
heer zint mye-ne terkh-ter. oont zee

These are my daughters. And you?

Conversational tip The most common way to ask a question in German is to invert the verb and the subject: "Sie haben" (you have) becomes "Haben Sie...?" (have you?, or do you have?). Similarly, "Sie möchten Kaffee" (you want coffee) becomes "Möchten Sie Kaffee?" (Do you want coffee?).

4 Useful phrases

Read these phrases aloud several times and try to memorize them. Conceal the German with the cover flap and test yourself.

Do you have any brothers? (formal)	**Haben Sie Brüder?** hah-ben zee brew-der
Do you have any brothers? (informal)	**Hast du Brüder?** husst doo brew-der

This is my husband.	**Hier ist mein Mann.** heer isst mine munn
That's my wife.	**Dort ist meine Frau.** dort isst mye-ne frow

Is that your sister? (formal)	**Ist das Ihre Schwester?** isst duss ee-re shvess-ter
Is that your sister? (informal)	**Ist das deine Schwester?** isst duss dye-ne shvess-ter

5 Say it

Do you have any brothers and sisters? (formal)

Do you have any children? (informal)

I don't have any sisters.

This is my wife.

Nein, aber ich habe einen Stiefsohn. nine, ah-ber ikh hah-be ie-nen shteef-zohn

No, but I have a stepson.

1 Warm up

Say "See you soon."
(pp.8–9)

Say "I am married"
and "I have a wife."
(pp.10–11 and
pp.12–13)

Sein und haben
To be and to have

German verbs have more forms than
English ones, so learn them carefully.
The verbs **sein** (*to be*) and **haben** (*to
have*) are used in many expressions,
often differently from English. For
example, in English you say "I'm
hungry," but in German you say **Ich
habe Hunger** (literally, *I have hunger*).

2 Sein: to be

Familiarize yourself with the different forms of **sein** (*to be*). Use the
cover flaps to test yourself and, when you are confident, practice the
sample sentences below.

ich bin ikh bin	*I am*
du bist doo bisst	*you are (informal, singular)*
er/sie/es ist air/zee/ess isst	*he/she/it is*
wir sind veer zint	*we are*
ihr seid eer ziet	*you are (informal, plural)*
sie sind/Sie sind zee zint	*they are/you are (formal)*

Ich bin Engländerin.
ikh bin ang-lan-darin
I'm English.

Ich bin müde. ikh bin mew-de	*I'm tired.*
Du bist/Sie sind pünktlich. doo bisst/zee zint pewnkt-likh	*You're on time.*
Ist sie glücklich? isst zee glewk-likh	*Is she happy?*
Wir sind Deutsche. veer zint doitche	*We're German.*

3 Haben

Learn this verb and the sample sentences. Use the flap to test yourself.

I have	**ich habe** ikh hah-be
you have (informal, singular)	**du hast** doo husst
he/she/it has	**er/sie/es hat** air/zee/ess hut
we have	**wir haben** veer hah-ben
you have (informal, plural)	**ihr habt** eer hahpt
they have/you have (formal)	**sie haben/Sie haben** zee hah-ben

Haben Sie Brokkoli?
hah-ben zee brokolee
Do you have any broccoli?

He has a meeting.	**Er hat eine Besprechung.** air hut ie-ne be-shpre-khoong
Do you have a cell phone?	**Haben Sie ein Handy?** hah-ben zee ine han-di
They have a half-brother.	**Sie haben einen Halbbruder.** zee hah-ben ie-nen hulp-broo-der

4 Negatives

The most common way to make a sentence negative in German is to put **nicht** (*not*) in front of the word that is negated, much as in English: **Wir sind nicht verheiratet** (*We are not married*). Note the following special negative constructions: *not a/not any* becomes **kein/keine**, *not ever/never* becomes **nie**, and *not anywhere/nowhere* becomes **nirgendwo**.

das Fahrrad
duss fahr-raht
bicycle

I'm not tired.	**Ich bin nicht müde.** ikh bin nikht mew-de
He's not married.	**Er ist nicht verheiratet.** air isst nikht fer-hye-rah-tet
We don't have any children.	**Wir haben keine Kinder.** veer hah-ben kye-ne kin-der

Ich habe kein Auto.
ikh hah-be kine ow-to
I don't have a car.

Wiederholung
Review and repeat

Antworten
Answers
Cover with flap

1 How many?

1 **drei**
drie

2 **neun**
noyn

3 **vier**
feer

4 **zwei**
tsvie

5 **acht**
akht

6 **zehn**
tsayn

7 **fünf**
fewnf

8 **sieben**
zee-ben

9 **sechs**
zeks

2 Hello

1 **Guten Tag. Ich heiße... [your name].**
goo-ten tahk. ikh high-se...

2 **Freut mich.**
froyt mikh

3 **Ja, und ich habe zwei Söhne. Und Sie?**
yah, oont ikh hah-be tsvie zer-ne. Oont zee?

4 **Auf Wiedersehen. Bis morgen.**
owf vee-der-zay-en. biss mor-gen

1 How many?

Conceal the answers with the cover flap. Then say these numbers in German. Check to see if you remembered correctly.

2 Hello

You meet someone in a formal situation. Join in the conversation, replying in German according to the English prompts.

Guten Tag. Ich heiße Claudia.
1 *Answer the greeting and give your name.*

Das ist mein Mann, Norbert.
2 *Say "Pleased to meet you."*

Sind Sie verheiratet?
3 *Say "Yes, and I have two sons. And you?"*

Wir haben drei Töchter.
4 *Say "Goodbye. See you tomorrow."*

3 To have or be

Fill in the blanks with the correct form of **haben** (*to have*) or **sein** (*to be*). Check to see if you remembered the German correctly.

1 Ich ____ verheiratet.

2 Sie *(she)* ____ müde.

3 Wir ____ Deutsche.

4 ____ Sie eine Besprechung?

5 Sie *(she)* ____ eine Schwägerin.

6 Ich ____ kein Handy.

7 ____ du glücklich?

8 Das ____ mein Mann.

3 To have or be

1 **bin**
   bin

2 **ist**
   isst

3 **sind**
   zint

4 **haben**
   hah-ben

5 **hat**
   hut

6 **habe**
   hah-be

7 **bist**
   bisst

8 **ist**
   isst

4 Family

Say the German for each of the numbered family members. Check to see if you remembered the German correctly.

grandfather ❶ brother ❷ ❸ sister ❹ father ❺ mother grandmother ❻ ❼ son ❽ daughter

4 Family

1 **der Großvater**
   dair groes-fah-ter

2 **der Bruder**
   dair broo-der

3 **die Schwester**
   dee shvess-ter

4 **der Vater**
   dair fah-ter

5 **die Mutter**
   dee moot-ter

6 **die Großmutter**
   dee groes-moot-ter

7 **der Sohn**
   dair zohn

8 **die Tochter**
   dee tokh-ter

Im Café
At the café

In a German **Café** the busiest time is the afternoon, when people stop for coffee and cake. Some savory dishes are also usually available, but the emphasis is on pastries and cakes.

1 Warm up

Count to ten.
(pp.10–11)

Say "hello" and
"goodbye." (pp.8–9)

Ask "Do you have a
brother?" (pp.12–13)

der Zucker
dair tsook-ker
sugar

2 Match and repeat

Familiarize yourself with the words below. Then test yourself by hiding the German with the cover flap. Practice the words on the picture also.

der Kaffee ohne Milch dair kuf-fay oh-ne milkh	*black coffee*
der Tee mit Milch dair tay mit milkh	*tea with milk*
das Gebäck duss ge-beck	*pastry*
das Sandwich duss zent-vitch	*sandwich*

der schwarze Tee
dair shvar-tse tay
black tea

Cultural tip Coffee is always served with milk and sugar, but tea drinkers should specify if they want milk ("mit Milch") or lemon ("mit Zitrone").

3 In conversation

Ich hätte gern eine Tasse Tee mit Milch.
ikh het-te gairn ie-ne tuss-se tay mit milkh

I would like a cup of tea with milk, please.

Sonst noch etwas?
zonsst nokh et-vuss

Anything else?

Haben Sie Kuchen?
hah-ben zee koo-khen

Do you have any cake?

4 Useful phrases

Practice these phrases and then test yourself using the cover flap.

ein Stück Kuchen
ine shtewck
koo-khen
slice of cake

der Kaffee
dair kuf-fay
(white) coffee

I'd like a cup of coffee, please.

Ich hätte gern eine Tasse Kaffee, bitte.
ikh het-te gairn ie-ne tuss-se kuf-fay, bit-te

Anything else?

Sonst noch etwas?
zonsst nokh et-vuss

Yes, a Danish pastry, please.

Ja, ein Teilchen, bitte.
yah, ine tile-khen, bit-te

How much is that?

Was macht das?
vuss mukht duss

Ja, selbstverständlich.
yah, zelpst-fer-shtend-likh

Yes, certainly.

Danke. Was macht das?
dun-ke. vuss mukht duss

Thank you. How much is that?

Vier Euro, bitte.
feer oy-roe, bit-te

Four euros, please.

1 Warm up

How do you say "I'd like"? (pp.18–19)

Say "I don't have a brother." (pp.14–15)

Is "der" masculine or feminine? When do you use "die"? (pp.10–11)

Im Restaurant
In the restaurant

There are many different eating places in Germany. A **Gaststätte** serves local or international dishes. In a **Gasthof** you'll get more home-style cooking. **Ratkeller**, in the basements of historic town halls, serve regional specialties. A **Weinstube** has local wine and snacks.

2 Words to remember

Memorize these words. Conceal the German with the cover flap and test yourself.

die Speisekarte dee shpie-ze-kar-te	*menu*
die Weinkarte dee vine-kar-te	*wine list*
die Vorspeisen dee for-shpie-zen	*appetizers*
die Hauptgerichte dee howpt-ge-rikh-te	*main courses*
der Nachtisch dair nahkh-tish	*desserts*
das Mittagessen duss mit-tahks-ess-sen	*lunch*
das Abendessen duss ah-bent-ess-sen	*dinner*
das Frühstück duss frew-shtewk	*breakfast*

cup ❼

knife ❻

❺ spoon   ❹ fork

3 In conversation

Einen Tisch für vier Personen.
ie-nen tish fewr feer pair-zoe-nen

A table for four.

Haben Sie reserviert?
hah-ben zee re-zair-veert

Do you have a reservation?

Ja, auf den Namen Schmidt.
yah, owf dayn nah-men shmitt

Yes, in the name of Schmidt.

4 Match and repeat

Look at the numbered items and match them with the vocabulary list at the side. Read the German words aloud. Now, conceal the list with the cover flap and test yourself.

glass ❶

❽ *saucer*

1	**das Glas**	duss glahss
2	**die Serviette**	dee zair-vee-ett-te
3	**der Teller**	dair tell-ler
4	**die Gabel**	dee gah-bell
5	**der Löffel**	dair lerff-fel
6	**das Messer**	duss mess-ser
7	**die Tasse**	dee tuss-se
8	**die Untertasse**	dee unter-tuss-se

5 Useful phrases

Learn these phrases and then test yourself using the cover flap to conceal the German.

napkin ❷

plate ❸

What do you have for dessert?	**Was haben Sie zum Nachtisch?** vuss hah-ben zee tsoom nahkh-tish
May I have the check, please?	**Könnte ich bitte die Rechnung haben.** kern-te ikh bit-te dee rekh-noong hah-ben

Welchen Tisch möchten Sie?
vel-khen tish merkh-ten zee

Which table would you like?

Am Fenster, bitte
um fens-ter, bit-te

Near the window, please.

Selbstverständlich. Folgen Sie mir.
zelpst-fer-shtend-likh. fol-gen zee meer

Of course. Follow me.

1 Warm up

What are "breakfast," "lunch," and "dinner" in German? (pp.20–1)

Say "I," "you" (informal, singular), "he," "she," "it," "we," "you" (formal), "they." (pp.14–15)

Mögen
To want

In this section, you will learn a verb, **mögen** (*to want*), which is essential to everyday conversation, as well as a useful polite expression, **ich hätte gern** (*I would like*). Remember to use this form when requesting something because **ich möchte** (*I want*) may sound too forceful.

2 Mögen: to want

Say the different forms of **mögen** (*to want*) aloud and practice the sample sentences below. Use the cover flaps to test yourself.

ich möchte ikh merkh-te	*I want*
du möchtest doo merkh-test	*you want (informal, singular)*
er/sie/es möchte air/zee/ess merkh-te	*he/she/it wants*
wir möchten veer merkh-ten	*we want*
ihr möchtet eer merkh-tet	*you want (informal, plural)*
sie möchten/Sie möchten zee merkh-ten	*they want/you want (formal)*
Möchtest du Wein? merkh-test doo vine	*Do you want some wine?*
Sie möchte ein neues Auto haben. zee merkh-te ine noy-es ow-to hah-ben	*She wants a new car.*
Wir möchten in Urlaub fahren. veer merkh-ten in oor-lowp fah-ren	*We want to go on vacation.*

Ich möchte Bonbons haben.
ikh merkh-te bom-bongs hah-ben
I want some candy.

■ **Conversational tip** In German you don't need to say "some" as in "We want some ice pops." Say just "Wir möchten Eis am Stiel haben." The phrase meaning "some" is "ein paar." It is generally used only when you want to imply some but not all, as in "Ich habe nur ein paar Bonbons gegessen."

3 Polite requests

It is polite to use the expression **ich hätte gern** (*I would like*) to explain what you would like.

I'd like a beer.

Ich hätte gern ein Bier.
ikh het-te gairn ine beer

I'd like a table for tonight.

Ich hätte gern einen Tisch für heute abend.
ikh het-te gairn ie-nen tish fewr hoy-te ah-bent

I'd like the menu.

Ich hätte gern die Speisekarte.
ikh het-te gairn dee shpie-ze-kar-te

4 Put into practice

Join in this conversation. Read the German beside the pictures on the left and then follow the instructions to make your reply in German. Test yourself by concealing the answers with the cover flap.

Guten Abend. Haben Sie reserviert?
goo-ten ah-bent. hah-ben zee re-zair-veert
Good evening. Do you have a reservation?

Say: No, but I would like a table for three.

Nein, aber ich hätte gern einen Tisch für drei Personen.
nine, ah-ber ikh het-te gairn ie-nen tish fewr drie per-zoe-nen

Sehr gut. Raucher oder Nichtraucher?
zair goot. row-kher oe-der nikht-row-kher
Fine. Smoking or nonsmoking?

Say: Nonsmoking, please.

Nichtraucher, bitte.
nikht-row-kher, bit-te

Say "I am tired."
(pp.14–15)

Ask "Do you have
pastries?" (pp.18–19)

Say "I'd like black
coffee." (pp.18–19)

Die Gerichte
Dishes

Germany is famous for its sausages
and meat dishes as well as its
sauerkraut and dumplings. Today's
restaurants, however, offer a wide
selection of international dishes.
Although traditionally the cuisine
is meat-based, many restaurants now
offer vegetarian dishes.

Cultural tip In most restaurants at
lunchtime you will usually have the choice of eating
a "Tagesgericht" (dish of the day) or of choosing
"à la carte" from the menu.

2 Match and repeat

Look at the numbered items and match them to the German words
in the panel on the left. Test yourself using the cover flap.

1 **das Gemüse**
duss ge-mew-ze

2 **das Obst**
duss opst

3 **der Käse**
dair kay-ze

4 **die Nüsse**
dee news-se

5 **die Suppe**
dee zoop-pe

6 **das Geflügel**
duss ge-flew-gel

7 **der Fisch**
dair fish

8 **die Nudeln**
dee noo-deln

9 **die Meeresfrüchte**
dee
mair-es-frewkh-te

10 **das Fleisch**
duss fliesh

1 vegetables

2 fruit

cheese **3**

5 soup

poultry **6**

8 pasta

9 seafood

3 Words to remember: cooking methods

Familiarize yourself with these words and then test yourself.

fried	**gebraten**	ge-brah-ten
grilled	**gegrillt**	ge-grillt
roasted	**geröstet**	ge-rerss-tet
boiled	**gekocht**	ge-kokht
steamed	**gedämpft**	ge-dempft
rare	**blutig**	bloo-tikh

Ich hätte mein Steak gern durchgebraten.
ikh het-te mine shtayk gairn doorkh-ge-brah-ten
I'd like my steak well done.

6 Say it

What is "Sauerbraten"?

I'm allergic to seafood.

I'd like fruit juice.

❹ *nuts*

❼ *fish*

❿ *meat*

4 Words to remember: drinks

Familiarize yourself with these words.

water	**das Wasser**	duss vuss-ser
sparkling water	**das Wasser mit Kohlensäure**	duss vuss-ser mit koe-len-zoy-re
still water	**das Wasser ohne Kohlensäure**	duss vuss-ser oe-ne koe-len-zoy-re
wine	**der Wein**	dair vine
fruit juice	**der Fruchtsaft**	dair frookht-zufft

5 Useful phrases

Learn these phrases and then test yourself.

I am a vegetarian.	**Ich bin Vegetarier/ Vegetarierin.**	ikh bin vay-ge-tah-ree-er/vay-ge-tah-ree-er-in
I am allergic to nuts.	**Ich bin allergisch gegen Nüsse.**	ikh bin ull-lair-gish gay-gen news-se
What is "Spätzle"?	**Was ist "Spätzle"?**	vuss isst shpets-le

Wiederholung
Review and repeat

Antworten
Answers
Cover with flap

1 What food?

1 **die Nüsse**
dee news-se

2 **die Meeresfrüchte**
dee mair-es-frewkh-te

3 **das Fleisch**
duss fliesh

4 **der Zucker**
dair tsook-ker

5 **das Glas**
duss glahss

1 What food?

Name the numbered items.

4 sugar

1 nuts

2 seafood

3 meat

glass 5

2 This is my...

1 **Das ist mein Ehemann.**
duss ist mine ay-emunn

2 **Hier ist meine Tochter.**
heer ist mye-ne tokh-ter

3 **Meine Kinder sind müde.**
mye-ne kin-der zint mew-de

2 This is my...

Say these phrases in German.
Use **mein** or **meine**.

1 *This is my husband.*

2 *Here is my daughter.*

3 *My children are tired.*

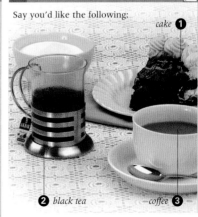

3 I'd like...

1 **Ich hätte gern Kuchen.**
ikh het-te gairn koo-khen

2 **Ich hätte gern einen schwarzen Tee.**
ikh het-te gairn ie-nen shvar-tsen tay

3 **Ich hätte gern einen Kaffee.**
ikh het-te gairn ie-nen kuf-fay

3 I'd like...

Say you'd like the following:

cake 1

2 black tea

coffee 3

6 *pasta*

knife 7

8 *cheese*

beer 10

9 *napkin*

1 What food?

6 **die Nudeln**
dee noo-deln

7 **das Messer**
duss mess-ser

8 **der Käse**
dair kay-ze

9 **die Serviette**
dee zair-vee-ett-te

10 **das Bier**
duss beer

4 Restaurant ▷

You arrive at a restaurant. Join in the conversation, replying in German following the English prompts.

Guten Tag.
1 *Ask for a table for six.*

Raucher oder Nichtraucher?
2 *Say: nonsmoking.*

Folgen Sie mir, bitte.
3 *Ask for the menu.*

Möchten Sie die Weinkarte?
4 *Say: No. Sparkling water, please.*

Bitte schön.
5 *Say: I don't have a glass.*

4 Restaurant

1 **Guten Tag. Ich hätte gern einen Tisch für sechs Personen.**
goo-ten tahk. ikh het-te gairn ie-nen tish fewr zeks pair-zoe-nen

2 **Nichtraucher.**
nikht-row-kher

3 **Die Speisekarte, bitte.**
dee shpie-ze-kar-te, bit-te

4 **Nein. Wasser mit Kohlensäure, bitte.**
nine. vuss-ser mit koe-len-zoy-re, bit-te

5 **Ich habe kein Glas.**
ikh hah-be kine glahss

1 Warm up

Say "he is" and "they are." (pp.14–15)

Say "he is not" and "they are not." (pp.14–15)

What is German for "the children"? (pp.10–11)

Die Tage und die Monate
Days and months

Days of the week and months are all masculine. **Die Woche** (*week*) is feminine. You use **im** with months: **im April** (*in April*), and **am** with days: **am Montag** (*on Monday*). You also use **am** with **Wochenende** (*weekend*).

2 Words to remember: days of the week

Familiarize yourself with these words and test yourself using the flap.

Montag moen-tahk	*Monday*
Dienstag deens-tahk	*Tuesday*
Mittwoch mit-vokh	*Wednesday*
Donnerstag don-ners-tahk	*Thursday*
Freitag frie-tahk	*Friday*
Samstag zumss-tahk	*Saturday*
Sonntag zonn-tahk	*Sunday*
heute hoy-te	*today*
morgen mor-gen	*tomorrow*
gestern guess-tern	*yesterday*

Morgen ist Montag.
mor-gen isst moen-tahk
Tomorrow is Monday.

3 Useful phrases: days

Learn these phrases and then test yourself using the cover flap.

Die Besprechung ist am Dienstag. dee be-shpre-khoong isst am deens-tahk	*The meeting is on Tuesday.*
Ich arbeite sonntags. ikh ar-bie-te zonn-tahks	*I work on Sundays.*

4 Words to remember: months

Familiarize yourself with these words and test yourself using the flap.

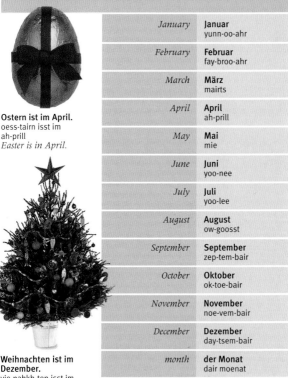

January	**Januar** yunn-oo-ahr	
February	**Februar** fay-broo-ahr	
March	**März** mairts	
April	**April** ah-prill	
May	**Mai** mie	
June	**Juni** yoo-nee	
July	**Juli** yoo-lee	
August	**August** ow-goosst	
September	**September** zep-tem-bair	
October	**Oktober** ok-toe-bair	
November	**November** noe-vem-bair	
December	**Dezember** day-tsem-bair	
month	**der Monat** dair moenat	
day	**der Tag** dair tahk	

Ostern ist im April.
oess-tairn isst im
ah-prill
Easter is in April.

Weihnachten ist im Dezember.
vie-nahkh-ten isst im
day-tsem-bair
Christmas is in December.

5 Useful phrases: months

Learn these phrases and then test yourself using the cover flap.

My children are on vacation in August.	**Meine Kinder haben im August Ferien.** mye-ne kin-der hah-ben im ow-goosst fay-ree-en

My birthday is in June.	**Mein Geburtstag ist im Juni.** mine ge-boorts-tahk isst im yoo-nee

Count in German from 1 to 10. (pp.10–11)

Say "I have a reservation." (pp.20–1)

Say "The meeting is on Wednesday." (pp.28–9)

Die Zeit und die Zahlen
Time and numbers

Germans use the 12-hour clock in everyday conversation and the 24-hour clock in official contexts such as timetables. Note that in German, five-thirty is expressed as **halb sechs** (literally, *half six*).

2 Words to remember: time

Familiarize yourself with these words.

ein Uhr ine oor	*one o'clock*
fünf nach eins fewnf nahkh ients	*five after one*
Viertel nach eins feer-tel nahkh ients	*quarter after one*
halb zwei hulp tsvie	*one-thirty*
ein Uhr zwanzig ine oor tsvun-tsik	*twenty after one*
Viertel vor zwei feer-tel for tsvie	*quarter to two*
zehn Minuten vor zwei tsayn mee-noo-ten for tsvie	*ten to two*

3 Useful phrases

Learn these phrases and then test yourself using the cover flap.

Wie spät ist es? vee shpayt isst es	*What time is it?*
Wann möchten Sie frühstücken? vunn merkh-ten zee frew-shtewk-ken	*What time do you want breakfast?*
Die Besprechung ist um 12 Uhr. dee be-shpre-khoong isst oom tsverlf oor	*The meeting is at noon.*

4 Words to remember: higher numbers

In German, units are said before tens, so 32 is **zweiunddreißig** (literally, *two-plus-thirty*). Because of this, Germans often write numbers starting at the right and working toward the left.

Ich habe viele Bücher.
ikh hah-be fee-le
bew-kher
I have many books.

Das macht fünfundachtzig Euro.
duss makht fewnf-oont-akh-tsik oy-roe
That's eighty-five euros.

eleven	**elf**	elf
twelve	**zwölf**	tsverlf
thirteen	**dreizehn**	drie-tsayn
fourteen	**vierzehn**	feer-tsayn
fifteen	**fünfzehn**	fewnf-tsayn
sixteen	**sechzehn**	zekh-tsayn
seventeen	**siebzehn**	zeep-tsayn
eighteen	**achtzehn**	akh-tsayn
nineteen	**neunzehn**	noyn-tsayn
twenty	**zwanzig**	tsvun-tsik
thirty	**dreißig**	drie-ssik
forty	**vierzig**	feer-tsik
fifty	**fünfzig**	fewnf-tsik
sixty	**sechzig**	zekh-tsik
seventy	**siebzig**	zeep-tsik
eighty	**achtzig**	akh-tsik
ninety	**neunzig**	noyn-tsik
one hundred	**hundert**	hoon-dairt
three hundred	**dreihundert**	drie-hoon-dairt
one thousand	**tausend**	tow-zent
ten thousand	**zehntausend**	tsayn-tow-zent
two hundred thousand	**zweihunderttausend**	tsvie-hoon-dairt-tow-zent
one million	**eine Million**	ie-ne mill-ee-oen

5 Say it

twenty-five

sixty-eight

eighty-four

ninety-one

It's five to ten.

It's eleven-thirty.

What time is lunch?

1 Warm up

Say the days of the week. (pp.28–9)

Say "It's three o'clock." (pp.30–1)

What's the German for "today," "tomorrow," and "yesterday"? (pp.28–9)

Die Termine
Appointments

Business in Germany is generally conducted more formally than in the US. Business associates generally call each other by their title and last name and use the formal form of "you," **Sie**. Appointments are usually fixed using the 24-hour clock, e.g., **fünfzehn Uhr** (3 pm).

2 Useful phrases

Learn these phrases and then test yourself.

Können wir uns morgen treffen? kern-en veer oons mor-gen treff-fen	*Can we meet tomorrow?*
Mit wem? mit vaym	*With whom?*
Wann sind Sie frei? vunn zint zee frie	*When are you free?*
Es tut mir Leid, ich bin beschäftigt. es toot meer liet, ikh bin be-sheff-tikht	*I'm sorry, I'm busy.*
Wie wär's mit Donnerstag? vee vairs mit don-ners-tahk	*How about Thursday?*
Das passt mir gut. duss pusst meer goot	*That's good for me.*

der Händedruck
dair hen-de-drook
handshake

Willkommen.
vil-komm-men
Welcome.

3 In conversation

Guten Tage. Ich habe einen Termin.
goo-ten tahk. ikh hah-be ie-nen terr-meen

Hello. I have an appointment.

Mit wem, bitte?
mit vaym, bit-te

With whom, please?

Mit Dieter Frenger.
mit dee-ter fren-ger

With Dieter Frenger.

4 Put into practice

Join in this conversation. Cover up the text on the right and say the answering part of the dialogue in German. Check your answers and repeat if necessary.

Können wir uns am Donnerstag treffen?
kernen veer oons am don-ners-tahk treff-fen
Shall we meet Thursday.

Say: *Sorry, I'm busy.*

Es tut mir Leid, ich bin beschäftigt.
es toot meer liet, ikh bin be-sheff-tikht

Wann sind Sie frei?
vunn zint zee frie
When are you free?

Say: *Tuesday afternoon.*

Dienstag Nachmittag.
deens-tahk nahkh-mit-tahk

Das passt mir gut.
duss pusst meer goot
That's good for me.

Ask: *At what time?*

Um wieviel Uhr?
oom vee-feel oor

Um sechzehn Uhr, wenn es Ihnen passt.
oom zekh-tsayn oor, venn ess ee-nen pusst
At 16:00 hours, if that's good for you.

Say: *It's good for me.*

Das passt mir gut.
duss pusst meer goot

Sehr gut. Um wieviel Uhr?
zair goot. oom vee-feel oor

Fine. What time?

Um fünfzehn Uhr, aber ich bin etwas verspätet.
oom fewnf-tsayn oor, ah-ber ikh bin et-vuss fer-shpay-tet

At 15:00 hours, but I'm a little late.

Kein Problem. Setzen Sie sich, bitte.
kine pro-blaym. zet-sen zee zikh, bit-te

Don't worry. Sit down, please.

1 Warm up

Say "I'm sorry."
(pp.32–3)

What is the German
for "I'd like an
appointment"?
(pp.32–3)

Ask "with whom?" in
German. (pp.32–3)

Am Telefon
On the telephone

Emergency phone numbers are:
Polizei (*police*) 110; **Feuerwehr** (*fire service*) 112; and **Rettungsdienst** (*ambulance*) 192 22. Directory assistance is 118 33 for domestic numbers, 118 34 for international, and 118 37 for an English-speaking service.

2 Match and repeat

Match the numbered items to the German.

1 **das Ladegerät**
  duss lah-de-ge-rayt

2 **das Telefon**
  duss tay-lay-foen

3 **der Anrufbeantworter**
  dair un-roof-bay-unt-vor-ter

4 **die Kopfhörer**
  dee kopf-her-er

5 **das Handy**
  duss han-di

6 **die Telefonkarte**
  dee tay-lay-foen-kar-te

❶ *charger*

❷ *telephone*

cell phone ❺

phone card ❻

❹ *headphones*

3 In conversation

Hallo. Elke Rubin am Apparat.
hul-lo. el-ke roo-been umm up-pa-raht

Hello. Elke Rubin speaking.

Guten Tag. Ich möchte bitte Peter Harnisch sprechen.
goo-ten tahk. ikh merkh-te bit-te peeter har-neesh shpre-khen

Hello. I'd like to speak to Peter Harnisch.

Mit wem spreche ich?
mit vaym shpre-khe ikh

Who's calling?

4 Useful phrases

Learn these phrases. Then test yourself using the cover flap.

I'd like an outside line.

Ich möchte einen Amtsanschluss.
ikh merkh-te ie-nen umts-un-shlooss

Ich möchte ein R-Gespräch.
ikh merkh-te ine air-geshprekh
I'd like to make a collect call.

 3 answering machine

I'd like to speak to Rita Wolbert.

Ich möchte mit Rita Wolbert sprechen.
ikh merkh-te mit ree-ta vol-bert shpre-khen

Can I leave a message?

Kann ich eine Nachricht hinterlassen?
kunn ikh ie-ne nahkh-rikht hin-ter-luss-sen

5 Say it

I'd like to speak to Mr. Braun.

Hello, Gaby Meyer speaking.

Sorry, I have the wrong number.

Es tut mir Leid, ich habe mich verwählt.
ess toot meer liet, ikh hah-be mikh fer-vaylt

Mit Norbert Lorenz von der Druckerei Knickmann.
mit nor-bert loe-rents fon dair drook-er-ie knick-munn

Norbert Lorenz of Knickmann Printers.

Es tut mir Leid. Es ist besetzt.
ess toot meer liet. ess isst be-zetst

I'm sorry. The line is busy.

Würden Sie ihn bitten, mich anzurufen?
vewr-den see een bit-ten, mikh un-tsoo-roo-fen

Can he call me back, please?

Wiederholung
Review and repeat

Antworten
Answers
Cover with flap

1 Sums

1 **sechzehn**
zekh-tsayn

2 **neununddreißig**
noyn-oont-drie-ssik

3 **dreiundfünfzig**
drie-oont-fewnf-tsik

4 **vierundsiebzig**
feer-oont-zeep-tsik

5 **neunundneunzig**
noyn-oont-noyn-tsik

6 **einundvierzig**
ine-oont-feer-tsik

1 Sums

Say the answers
to these sums
aloud in German.
Then check to see
if you remembered
correctly.

1 $10 + 6 = ?$

2 $14 + 25 = ?$

3 $66 - 13 = ?$

4 $40 + 34 = ?$

5 $90 + 9 = ?$

6 $46 - 5 = ?$

3 Telephones

What are the numbered
items in German?

cell phone ❶

phone card ❸

2 I want...

1 **möchten**
merkh-ten

2 **möchte**
merkh-te

3 **möchten**
merkh-ten

4 **möchtest**
merkh-test

5 **möchte**
merkh-te

6 **möchte**
merkh-te

2 I want...

Fill the gaps with
the correct form
of **mögen** (to want).

1 _____ Sie einen
Kaffee?

2 Sie *(singular)*
_____ in Urlaub
fahren.

3 Wir _____ einen Tisch für drei Personen.

4 Du _____ ein Bier.

5 Ich _____ Bonbons.

6 Er _____ Obst.

② *answering machine*

④ *telephone* *headphones* ⑤

3 Telephones

1 **das Handy**
duss han-di

2 **der Anrufbeantworter**
dair un-roof-bay-unt-vor-ter

3 **die Telefonkarte**
dee tay-lay-foen-kar-te

4 **das Telefon**
duss tay-lay-foen

5 **die Kopfhörer**
dee kopf-her-er

4 When?

What do these sentences mean?

1 **Ich habe einen Termin am Montag, den zwanzigsten Mai.**

2 **Mein Geburtstag ist im September.**

3 **Ich arbeite freitags.**

4 **Sie arbeiten nicht im August.**

4 When?

1 *I have an appointment on Monday, May 20.*

2 *My birthday is in September.*

3 *I work on Fridays.*

4 *They don't work in August.*

5 Time

Say these times in German.

5 Time

1 **ein Uhr**
ine oor

2 **fünf nach eins**
fewnf nahkh ients

3 **zwanzig Minuten nach eins**
tsvun-tsik mee-noo-ten nahkh ients

4 **halb zwei**
hulp tsvie

5 **Viertel nach eins**
feer-tel nahkh ients

6 **zehn Minuten vor zwei (Uhr)**
tsayn mee-noo-ten for tsvie (oor)

1 Warm up

Count to 100 in tens.
(pp.10–11, pp.30–1)

Ask "At what time?"
(pp.32–3)

Say "One-thirty."
(pp.30–1)

Am Fahrkartenschalter
At the ticket office

On German trains, children under the age of four travel free, and children from 4 to 11 years old pay half fare. There are also other concessions—for example, for senior citizens, groups, and weekend travel.

2 Words to remember

Learn these words and then test yourself.

der Bahnhof dair bahn-hoef	*station*
der Zug dair tsook	*train*
der Fahrplan dair fahr-plahn	*schedule*
die Fahrkarte dee fahr-kar-te	*ticket*
eine einfache Fahrkarte ie-ne ine-fa-khe fahr-kar-te	*one-way ticket*
eine Rückfahrkarte ie-ne rewck-fahr-kar-te	*round-trip ticket*
erster/zweiter Klasse airs-ter/tsvie-ter kluss-se	*first class/second class*

der Bahnsteig
dair bahn-shtiek
platform

das Schild
duss shilt
sign

Der Bahnhof ist überfüllt.
dair bahn-hoef isst ew-ber-fewllt
The station is crowded.

3 In conversation

Zwei Fahrkarten nach Berlin, bitte.
tsvie fahr-kar-ten nahkh bair-leen, bit-te

Two tickets to Berlin, please.

Rückfahrkarten?
rewck-fahr-kar-ten

Round-trip?

Ja. Muss ich die Sitze reservieren?
yah. mooss ikh dee zit-se re-zair-vee-ren

Yes. Do I need to reserve seats?

4 Useful phrases

Learn these phrases and then test yourself using the cover flap.

Der Zug hat zehn Minuten Verspätung.
dair tsook hut tsayn mee-noo-ten fer-shpay-toong
The train is ten minutes late.

der Fahrgast
dair fahr-gust
passenger

How much is a ticket to Cologne?	**Was kostet eine Fahrkarte nach Köln?** vuss kos-tet ie-ne fahr-kar-te nahkh kerln
Can I pay by credit card?	**Kann ich mit Kreditkarte zahlen?** kunn ikh mit kray-deet-kar-te tsah-len
Do I have to change trains?	**Muss ich umsteigen?** mooss ikh oomm-shtie-gen
Which platform does the train leave from?	**Von welchem Bahnsteig fährt der Zug ab?** fon vel-khem bahn-shtiek fairt dair tsook up
Are there any discounts?	**Gibt es Ermäßigungen?** geept ess er-mays-si-goong-en
What time does the train to Dresden leave?	**Wann fährt der Zug nach Dresden ab?** vunn fairt dair tsook nahkh dres-den up

5 Say it

Which platform does the train to Leipzig leave from?

Three round-trip tickets to Hamburg, please.

Cultural tip Most stations have automatic ticket machines (Fahrkartenautomaten). If you are in a hurry, you can buy tickets on the train, but you won't be able to get any discounts.

Nein. Vierzig Euro, bitte.
nine. feer-tsik oy-roe, bit-te

No. Forty euros, please.

Nehmen Sie Kreditkarten?
nay-men zee kray-deet-kar-ten

Do you take credit cards?

Ja. Der Zug fährt auf Bahnsteig zehn ab.
yah. dair tsook fairt owf bahn-shtiek tsayn up

Yes. The train leaves from platform ten.

1 Warm up

Say "train" in German. (pp.38–9)

What does "von welchem Bahnsteig fährt der Zug ab?" mean? (pp.38–9)

Ask "When are you free?" (pp.32–3)

Gehen und nehmen
To go and to take

Gehen (*to go*) and **nehmen** (*to take*) are essential verbs in German and form part of many useful expressions. Note that these verbs are not always used in the same way as in English and you need to learn phrases individually.

2 Gehen: to go

Say the different forms of **gehen** (*to go*) aloud. Use the cover flaps to test yourself and, when you are confident, practice the sample sentences below.

ich gehe ikh gay-e	*I go*
du gehst doo gayst	*you go (informal, singular)*
er/sie/es geht air/zee/ess gayt	*he/she/it goes*
wir gehen veer gay-en	*we go*
ihr geht eer gayt	*you go (informal, plural)*
sie gehen/Sie gehen zee gay-en	*they go/you go (formal)*
Wo gehen Sie hin? voe gay-en zee hin	*Where are you going?*
Ich gehe nach Bonn. ikh gay-e nahkh bonn	*I'm going to Bonn.*
Wie geht es Ihnen? vee gayt ess ee-nen	*How are you?*

Ich gehe zum Brandenburger Tor.
ikh gay-e tsoom brun-den-boor-ger tor
I'm going to the Brandenburg Gate.

Conversational tip German uses the same verb form for both "I go" and "I am going." There is no equivalent of the English present continuous tense, which uses the "-ing" ending. For example, "Ich gehe nach Hamburg" means both "I am going to Hamburg" and "I go to Hamburg." The same is true of other verbs: "Ich nehme den Zug" (I am taking the train/I take the train).

3 Nehmen: to take

Say the different forms of **nehmen** (*to take*) aloud and then practice the sample sentences below. Use the cover flaps to test yourself.

I take	**ich nehme** ikh nay-me
you take (informal, singular)	**du nimmst** doo nimmst
he/she/it takes	**er/sie/es nimmt** air/zee/ess nimmt
we take	**wir nehmen** veer nay-men
you take (informal, plural)	**ihr nehmt** eer naymt
they take/you take (formal)	**sie nehmen/Sie nehmen** zee nay-men

Ich nehme die Straßenbahn jeden Tag.
ikh nay-me dee shtrahs-sen-bahn yay-den tahk
I take the tram every day.

I don't want to take a taxi.	**Ich möchte kein Taxi nehmen.** ikh merkh-te kine tuck-see nay-men

Take the first left.	**Nehmen Sie die erste Straße links.** nay-men zee dee airs-te shtrahs-se links

He'll have the roast venison.	**Er nimmt den Rehbraten.** air nimmt dayn ray-brah-ten

4 Put into practice

Cover the text on the right and complete the dialogue in German.

Wo gehen Sie hin?
voe gay-en zee hin
Where are you going?

Say: I'm going to the station.

Ich gehe zum Bahnhof.
ikh gay-e tsoom bahn-hoef

Möchten Sie die U-Bahn nehmen?
merkh-ten zee dee oo-bahn nay-men
Do you want to take the metro?

Say: No, we want to go by bus.

Nein, wir wollen den Bus nehmen.
nine, veer vol-len dayn booss nay-men

Taxi, Bus und Bahn
Public transportation

The larger towns have underground trains (**U-Bahn**). Many also have over-ground trams (**Straßenbahn**) or express trains (**S-Bahn**). In most cases you need to buy and validate your ticket before you start the journey.

2 Words to remember

Familiarize yourself with these words.

der Bus dair booss	*bus (local)*
der Überlandbus dair ew-ber-lunt-booss	*bus (long-distance)*
der Busbahnhof dair booss-bahn-hoef	*bus station*
die Bushaltestelle dee booss-hal-te-shtel-le	*bus stop*
der Fahrpreis dair fahr-priess	*fare*
das Taxi duss tuck-see	*taxi*
der Taxistand dair tuck-see-shtunt	*taxi stand*
die U-Bahnstation dee oo-bahn-shta-tsee-oen	*subway station*

Hält der Bus Nummer hundertzwanzig hier?
helt dair booss noom-mer hoon-dairt-tsvun-tsik heer
Does the Route 120 bus stop here?

3 In conversation: taxi

Zum Flughafen, bitte.
tsoom flook-hah-fen, bit-te

The airport, please.

Jawohl, kein Problem.
yah-voel. kine pro-blaym

Yes, no problem.

Können Sie mich bitte hier absetzen?
ker-nen zee mikh bit-te heer up-zet-sen

Can you drop me here, please?

4 Useful phrases

Practice these phrases and then test yourself using the cover flap.

	I would like a taxi to the cathedral.	**Ich hätte gern ein Taxi zum Dom.** ikh het-te gairn ine tuck-see tsoom doem
	When is the next bus?	**Wann fährt der nächste Bus?** vunn fairt dair nekh-ste booss
	How do you get to the museum?	**Wie komme ich zum Museum?** vee kom-me ikh tsoom moo-zay-oom
	How long is the trip?	**Wie lange dauert die Fahrt?** vee lan-ge dow-airt dee fahrt
	Please wait for me.	**Bitte warten Sie auf mich.** bit-te vahr-ten zee owf mikh

Cultural tip Taxis in Germany all have meters. You can hail a taxi in the street when the lights are switched on, board one at a taxi stand, or call for a taxi from your hotel or private address. Round up the fare to tip the driver.

6 Say it

Do you go near the train station?

The bus station, please.

When's the next coach to Kiel?

5 In conversation: bus

Fahren Sie in der Nähe vom Museum entlang?
fah-ren zee in dair nay-e fom moo-zay-oom ent-lung

Do you go near the museum?

Ja. Das kostet achtzig Cent.
yah. duss kos-tet akh-tsik tsent

Yes. That's 80 cents.

Können Sie mir sagen, wann wir da sind?
ker-nen zee meer zah-gen, vunn veer dah zind

Can you tell me when we arrive?

1 Warm up

How do you say "I have..."? (pp.14–15)

Say "my father," "my sister," and "my parents." (pp.10–11 and pp.12–13)

Say "I'm going to Berlin." (pp.40–1)

Auf der Straße
On the road

German **Autobahnen** (*expressways*) are fast, but on many stretches there is now a speed limit of 80 mph (130 km/h). They are marked with the letter "A" on a blue sign; international expressways are "E" (**Europastraße**) on a green sign, and main roads "B" (**Bundesstraße**) on a white sign.

2 Match and repeat

Match the numbered items to the list on the left, then test yourself.

1 **der Kofferraum**
dair kof-fer-rowm

2 **die Windschutz-scheibe**
dee vint-shoots-shie-be

3 **die Motorhaube**
dee mo-tor-how-be

4 **der Reifen**
dair rie-fen

5 **das Rad**
duss raht

6 **die Tür**
dee tewr

7 **die Stoßstange**
dee shtoess-shtange

8 **die Scheinwerfer**
dee shien-vair-fer

> ▬ **Cultural tip** In Germany it is mandatory to carry with you in the car at all times your driver's license, car registration document, and a valid insurance certificate.

1 *trunk*

4 *tire*

5 *wheel*   **6** *door*   *bumper* **7**

3 Road signs

die Einbahnstraße
dee ine-bahn-shtrah-se

One way

der Kreisverkehr
dair kries-fer-kair

Roundabout

Vorfahrt achten
for-fahrt akh-ten

Yield

4 Useful phrases

Learn these phrases and then test yourself using the cover flap.

My turn signal isn't working.	**Mein Blinker funktioniert nicht.** mine blin-ker foonk-tsee-oe-neert nikht
Fill it up, please.	**Volltanken, bitte.** foll-tan-ken, bit-te

5 Words to remember

Familiarize yourself with these words, then test yourself using the flap.

6 Say it

My gearbox isn't working.

I have a flat tire.

2 *windshield*

3 *hood*

headlights **8**

gasoline	**das Benzin** duss ben-tseen
diesel	**der Diesel** dair dee-zel
oil	**das Öl** duss erl
engine	**der Motor** dair moe-tor
gearbox	**das Getriebe** duss ge-tree-be
turn signal	**der Blinker** dair blin-ker
flat tire	**ein Platten** ine plutt-ten
exhaust	**der Auspuff** dair ows-pooff
driver's license	**der Führerschein** dair few-rer-shien

die Vorfahrtstraße
dee for-fahrt-shtrah-se

Priority route

Einfahrt verboten
ine-fahrt fer-boe-ten

No entry

Parken verboten
par-ken fer-boe-ten

No parking

Wiederholung
Review and repeat

1 Transportation

1 **der Bus**
dair booss

2 **das Taxi**
duss tuk-see

3 **das Auto**
duss ow-toe

4 **das Fahrrad**
duss fahr-raht

5 **der Zug**
dair tsook

1 Transportation

Name these forms of transportation in German.

bus 1

2 *taxi*

5 *train*

2 Go and take

1 **gehe**
gay-e

2 **geht**
gayt

3 **nehme**
nay-me

4 **gehen**
gay-en

5 **nehmen**
nay-men

6 **gehen**
gay-en

2 Go and take

Use the correct form of the verb in brackets.

1 Ich _____ zum Bahnhof. (gehen)

2 Wie _____ es dir? (gehen)

3 Ich _____ den Rehbraten. (nehmen)

4 Wir _____ nach Berlin. (gehen)

5 _____ Sie die erste Straße links. (nehmen)

6 Wo _____ Sie hin? (gehen)

3 car

4 bicycle

3 Du or Sie?

Use the correct form of you.

1 *You are in a café. Ask "Do you have any cake?"*

2 *You are with a friend. Ask "Do you want a beer?"*

3 *A stranger approaches you at your company's reception desk. Ask "Do you have an appointment?"*

4 *You are on the bus. Ask "Do you go near the station?"*

5 *Ask your mother where she's going.*

3 Du or Sie?

1 **Haben Sie Kuchen?**
hah-ben zee koo-khen

2 **Möchtest du ein Bier?**
merkh-test doo ine beer

3 **Haben Sie einen Termin?**
hah-ben zee ie-nen terr-meen

4 **Fahren Sie in der Nähe vom Bahnhof entlang?**
fah-ren zee in dair nay-e fom bahn-hoef ent-lung

5 **Wo gehst du hin?**
voe gayst doo hin

4 Tickets

You're buying tickets at a train station. Follow the conversation, replying in German following the numbered English prompts.

Kann ich Ihnen helfen?
1 *I'd like two tickets to Berlin.*

Rückfahrkarte oder einfach?
2 *Round-trip, please.*

Bitte schön. Fünfzig Euro, bitte.
3 *What time does the train leave?*

Um dreizehn Uhr zehn.
4 *What platform does the train leave from?*

Bahnsteig sieben.
5 *Thank you very much. Goodbye.*

4 Tickets

1 **Ich hätte gern zwei Fahrkarten nach Berlin.**
ikh het-te gairn tsvie fahr-kar-ten nahkh bair-leen

2 **Rückfahrkarte, bitte.**
rewck-fahr-kar-te, bit-te

3 **Wann fährt der Zug ab?**
vunn fairt dair tsook up

4 **Von welchem Bahnsteig fährt der Zug ab?**
fon vel-khem bahn-shtiek fairt dair tsook up

5 **Vielen Dank. Auf Wiedersehen.**
fee-len dunk. owf vee-der-zay-en

1 Warm up

Ask "How do you get to the musuem?"
(pp.42–3)

Say "I want to take the bus" and "I don't want to take a taxi."
(pp.40–1)

In der Stadt
Around town

Most German towns still have a market day and a thriving community of small shops. Even small villages tend to have a mayor and a town hall. Parking is usually regulated. Look for blue parking zones, where you can park your car for a limited time without charge.

2 Match and repeat

Match the numbered locations to the words in the panel.

1 **das Rathaus**
  duss raht-hows

2 **die Brücke**
  dee brew-ke

3 **die Kirche**
  dee keer-khe

4 **der Parkplatz**
  dair park-pluts

5 **das Stadtzentrum**
  duss shtutt-tsen-troom

6 **der Platz**
  dair pluts

7 **die Kunstgalerie**
  dee koonst-gal-le-ree

8 **das Museum**
  duss moo-zay-oom

❶ *town hall*

❷ *bridge*

church ❸

square ❻

3 Words to remember

Familiarize yourself with these words.

die Tankstelle dee tunk-shtel-le	*gas station*
das Verkehrsbüro duss fer-kairs-bew-roe	*tourist information*
die Werkstatt dee vairk-shtutt	*car repairs*
das Schwimmbad duss shvim-bad	*swimming pool*
die Bibliothek dee beeb-lee-o-tayk	*library*

❼ *art gallery*

4 Useful phrases

Learn these phrases and then test yourself using the cover flap.

A useful expression for asking about public amenities is **es gibt** (*there is*). Notice that some words are often contracted in German—for example, **in dem** (*in the*) is contracted to **im**; **zu dem** (*to the,* masculine and neuter) becomes **zum**; and **zu der** (*to the,* feminine) contracts to **zur**.

Is there an art gallery in town?	**Gibt es eine Kunstgalerie in der Stadt?** geept es ie-ne koonst-gal-le-ree in dair shtutt
Is it far from here?	**Ist das weit von hier?** isst duss viet fon heer
There is a swimming pool near the bridge.	**Es gibt ein Schwimm-bad bei der Brücke.** es geept ien shvim-bad bie dair brew-ke
There isn't a library.	**Es gibt keine Bibliothek.** es geept kie-ne beeb-lee-o-tayk

4 *parking lot*

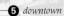

5 *downtown*

5 Put into practice

Join in this conversation. Conceal the text on the right with the cover flap and complete the dialogue in German. Check your answers and repeat if necessary.

Kann ich Ihnen helfen? kunn ikh ee-nen hel-fen *Can I help you?* Ask: *Is there a library in town?*	**Gibt es in der Stadt eine Bibliothek?** geept es in dair shtutt ie-ne beeb-lee-o-tayk
Nein, aber es gibt ein Museum. nine, ah-ber es geept ine moo-zay-oom *No, but there's a museum.* Ask: *How do I get to the museum?*	**Wie komme ich zum Museum?** vee kom-me ikh tsoom moo-zay-oom
Es ist dort. es isst dort *It's over there.* Say: *Thank you very much.*	**Vielen Dank.** fee-len dunk

8 *museum*

Die Wegbeschreibung
Finding your way

1 Warm up

How do you say "near the station"? (pp.42–3)

Say "Take the first left." (pp.40–1)

Ask "Where are you going?" (pp.40–1)

In German you use **gehen** (*to go*) when talking about going somewhere on foot but **fahren** (*to drive*) when in a car. So "go left" is **Gehen Sie nach links** if you are on foot, but **Fahren Sie nach links** if you are traveling in a car.

2 Useful phrases

Learn these phrases and then test yourself.

Gehen Sie nach links/rechts gay-en zee nahkh links/rekhts	*go left/right*
auf der linken Seite/ rechten Seite owf dair lin-ken zie-te/rekh-ten zie-te	*on the left side/ right side*
geradeaus (weiter) ge-rah-de-ows (vieter)	*(continue) straight ahead*
Wie komme ich zum Schwimmbad? vee kom-me ikh tsoom shvim-bad	*How do I get to the swimming pool?*
die erste (Straße) links dee airs-te (shtrah-se) links	*first (street) on the left*

die Bibliothek
dee beeb-lee-o-tayk
library

die Fußgängerzone
dee foos-gen-ger-tsoe-ne
pedestrian zone

Gehen Sie am Hauptplatz nach links.
gay-en zee am howpt-pluts nahkh links
Turn left at the main square.

3 In conversation

Gibt es ein Restaurant in der Stadt?
geept es ine res-to-rung in der shtutt

Is there a restaurant in town?

Ja, am Bahnhof.
yah, um bahn-hoef

Yes, near the station.

Wie komme ich zum Bahnhof?
vee kom-me ikh tsoom bahn-hoef

How do I get to the station?

4 Words to remember

Familiarize yourself with these words and test yourself using the flap.

Ich habe mich verlaufen.
ikh hah-be mikh
fer-low-fen
I'm lost.

traffic lights	**die Ampel** dee um-pel
corner	**die Ecke** dee ek-ke
street/road	**die Straße** dee shtrah-se
main road	**die Hauptstraße** dee howpt-shtrah-se
at the end of the street	**am Ende der Straße** um en-de dair shtrah-se
(town) map	**der Stadtplan** dair shtutt-plahn
overpass	**die Überführung** dee ew-ber-few-roong
opposite	**gegenüber** gay-gen-ew-ber

der Brunnen
dair broon-nen
fountain

Wir sind hier.
veer zind heer
We are here.

5 Say it

Go right at the end of the street.

It's opposite the museum.

It's ten minutes by bus.

Gehen Sie an der Ampel nach links.
gay-en zee un dair um-pel nahkh links

Go left at the traffic lights.

Ist es weit?
isst es viet

Is it far?

Nein, es ist fünf Minuten zu Fuß.
nine, es isst fewnf mee-noo-ten tsoo fooss

No, it's five minutes on foot.

1 Warm up

Say the days of the week in German. (pp.28–9)

How do you say "at six o'clock"? (pp.30–1)

Ask "What time is it?" (pp.30–1)

Die Besichtigung
Sightseeing

Museums tend to be open all day, but have more restricted opening hours in smaller villages where they are often closed on Sundays. Once a week, usually on Wednesdays or Thursdays, the larger museums will stay open later, while many are closed on Mondays and on public holidays.

2 Words to remember

Familiarize yourself with these words and test yourself using the flap.

der Führer dair few-rer	*guidebook*
die Eintrittskarte dee ine-trits-kar-te	*admission ticket*
die Öffnungszeiten dee erff-noongs-tsie-ten	*opening times*
der Feiertag dair fie-er-tahk	*public holiday*
die Ermäßigung dee er-mes-see-goong	*discount*

die Führung
dee few-roong
guided tour

> **Cultural tip** Germany observes a number of religious holidays in addition to Christmas and Easter—for example, Whit Monday and Ascension Day. May 1 is always a public holiday, whatever day of the week it falls on. There are also additional regional holidays.

3 In conversation

Sind Sie heute Nachmittag geöffnet?
zint zee hoy-te nahkh-mit-tahk ge-erff-net

Are you open this afternoon?

Ja, aber wir schließen um sechzehn Uhr.
yah, ah-ber veer shliee-sen oom zekh-tsayn oor

Yes, but we close at 4 pm.

Gibt es Zugang für Rollstuhlfahrer?
geept es tsoo-gung fewr roll-shtool-fah-rer

Do you have wheelchair access?

4 Useful phrases

Learn these phrases and then test yourself using the cover flap.

Öffnungszeiten:
Di.- Fr. 11-18 Uhr
Sa.+ So. 11-16 Uhr
(Montags geschlossen)

What time do you open/close?

Wann öffnen/ schließen Sie?
vunn erf-nen/shlee-sen zee

Where are the restrooms?

Wo sind die Toiletten?
voe zind dee twah-let-ten

Is there wheelchair access?

Gibt es Zugang für Rollstuhlfahrer?
geept es tsoo-gung fewr roll-shtool-fah-rer

5 Put into practice

Cover the text on the right and complete the dialogue in German.

Das Museum ist geschlossen.
duss moo-zay-oom isst ge-shlos-sen
The museum is closed.

Ask: Are you open on Mondays?

Sind Sie am Montag geöffnet?
zint zee um moen-tahk ge-erff-net

Ja, aber wir schließen früh.
yah, ah-ber veer shlee-sen frew
Yes, but we close early.

Ask: At what time?

Um wieviel Uhr?
oom vee-feel oor

Ja, da drüben ist ein Fahrstuhl.
yah, dar drew-ben isst ine fahr-shtool

Yes, there's an elevator over there.

Danke, ich hätte gern vier Eintrittskarten.
dun-ke, ikh het-te gairn feer ine-trits-kar-ten

Thank you, I'd like four admission tickets.

Bitte sehr, und der Führer ist gratis.
bit-te zair, oont dair few-rer isst grah-tis

Here you are, and the guidebook is free.

1 Warm up

Say "You're on time."
(pp.14–15)

What's the German for
"ticket"? (pp.38–9)

Say "I am going to
New York." (pp.40–1)

Im Flughafen
At the airport

Although the airport environment is
largely signposted in English, it will
sometimes be useful to be able to ask
your way around the terminal in
German. It's a good idea to make sure
you have a few one-euro coins when
you arrive at the airport; you may
need to pay for a baggage cart.

2 Words to remember

Familiarize yourself with these words and test yourself using the flap.

die Gepäckausgabe dee ge-peck-ows- gah-be	*baggage claim*
der Abflug dair up-flook	*departures*
die Ankunft dee un-koonft	*arrivals*
der Zoll dair tsoll	*customs*
die Passkontrolle dee puss-kon-trol-le	*passport control*
das Terminal duss terr-mee-nahl	*terminal*
der Flugsteig dair flook-shtiek	*gate*
die Flugnummer dee flook-noom-mer	*flight number*

**Von welchem
Flugsteig geht der
Flug 23?**
fon vel-khem flook-
shtiek gayt dair flook
drie-oont-tsvun-tsik
*What gate does flight
23 leave from?*

3 Useful phrases

Learn these phrases and then test yourself using the cover flap.

Geht der Flug nach Hannover pünktlich ab? gayt dair flook nahkh hun-no-fer pewnkt-likh up	*Will the flight for Hanover leave on time?*
Ich kann mein Gepäck nicht finden. ikh kunn mine ge-peck nikht fin-den	*I can't find my baggage.*

4 Put into practice

Join in this conversation. Read the German on the left and follow
the instructions to make your reply. Then test yourself by concealing
the answers with the cover flap.

**Guten Abend. Kann
ich Ihnen helfen?**
goo-ten ah-bent. kunn
ikh ee-nen hel-fen
Hello, can I help you?

*Ask: Is the flight to
Cologne on time?*

**Geht der Flug nach
Köln pünktlich ab?**
gayt dair flook nahkh
kerln pewnkt-likh up

Ja.
yah
Yes.

*Ask: What gate does
it leave from?*

**Von welchem
Flugsteig geht er ab?**
fon vel-khem flook-
shtiek gayt air up

5 Match and repeat

Match the numbered items to the German words in the panel.

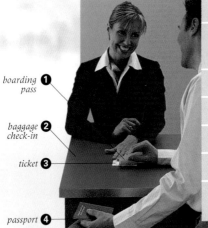

boarding
pass **1**

baggage **2**
check-in

ticket **3**

passport **4**

5 suitcase   **6** carry-on luggage   **7** cart

1 **die Bordkarte**
dee bort-kar-te

2 **der Abfertigungs-
schalter**
dair up-fer-ti-goongs-
shull-ter

3 **das Flugticket**
duss flook-tik-ket

4 **der Pass**
dair puss

5 **der Koffer**
dair kof-fer

6 **das Handgepäck**
duss hunt-ge-peck

7 **der Kofferkuli**
dair kof-fer-koo-li

Antworten
Answers
Cover with flap

Wiederholung
Review and repeat

1 Places

1 Places

1 **das Museum**
duss moo-zay-oom

2 **das Rathaus**
duss raht-hows

3 **die Brücke**
dee brew-ke

4 **die Kunstgalerie**
dee koonst-gal-le-ree

5 **der Parkplatz**
dair park-pluts

6 **der Dom**
dair doem

7 **der Platz**
dair pluts

1 Places

Name the numbered places in German.

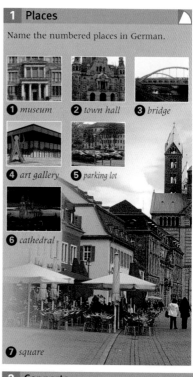

1 *museum* 2 *town hall* 3 *bridge*

4 *art gallery* 5 *parking lot*

6 *cathedral*

7 *square*

2 Car parts

2 Car parts

1 **die Windschutzscheibe**
dee vint-shoots-shie-be

2 **der Blinker**
dair blin-ker

3 **die Motorhaube**
dee mo-tor-how-be

4 **der Reifen**
dair rie-fen

5 **die Tür**
dee tewr

6 **die Stoßstange**
dee shtoess-shtange

2 Car parts

Name these car parts in German.

windshield 1

5 *door*

4 *tire*

3 Questions

Ask the questions in German that match the following answers:

1 Der zbus fährt um acht Uhr ab.

2 Kaffee, das macht zwei Euro fünfzig.

3 Nein, ich möchte keinen Wein.

4 Der Zug fährt von Bahnsteig fünf ab.

5 Wir fahren nach Leipzig.

6 Nein, es ist drei Minuten zu Fuß.

3 Questions

1 **Wann fährt der Überlandbus ab?**
vunn fairt dair ewber-lunt-boos up

2 **Was kostet der Kaffee?**
vuss kos-tet dair kuf-fay

3 **Möchten Sie Wein?**
merkh-ten zee vine

4 **Von welchem Bahnsteig fährt der Zug ab?**
fon vel-khem bahn-shtiek fairt dair tsook up

5 **Wo fahren Sie hin?**
voe fah-ren zee hin

6 **Ist es weit?**
isst es viet

② *turn signal*

③ *hood*

bumper ⑥

4 Verbs

Choose the correct verb and form to fill in the blanks.

1 Ich ____ Deutsche(r).

2 Wir ____ mit dem Bus.

3 Sie *(she)* ____ nach Dresden.

4 Er ____ drei Töchter.

5 ____ du Tee?

6 Wie viele Kinder ____ Sie?

7 Wo ____ die Toiletten?

4 Verbs

1 **bin**
bin

2 **fahren**
fah-ren

3 **geht**
gayt

4 **hat**
hut

5 **möchtest**
merkh-test

6 **haben**
hah-ben

7 **sind**
zint

1 Warm up

How do you ask in German "Do you take credit cards?" (pp.38–9)

Ask "How much is that?" (pp.18–19)

How do you ask "Do you have children?" (pp.12–13)

Die Zimmer-reservierung
Booking a room

There are different types of accommodation: **das Hotel**, rated by one to five stars; **die Pension** or **der Gasthof**, which are traditional inns; and private accommodation where signs advertise **Zimmer frei** or **Fremdenzimmer**.

2 Useful phrases

Practice these phrases and then test yourself by concealing the German on the left with the cover flap.

Ist das Frühstück inbegriffen?
isst duss frew-shtewk in-be-grif-fen

Is breakfast included?

Sind Tiere zugelassen?
zint tee-re tsoo-ge-luss-sen

Are pets allowed?

Haben Sie Zimmerservice?
hah-ben zee tsim-mer-sair-vis

Do you have room service?

Wann muss ich das Zimmer freimachen?
vunn mooss ikh duss tsim-mer frie-ma-khen

When must I check out?

3 In conversation

Haben Sie noch Zimmer frei?
hah-ben zee nokh tsim-mer frie

Do you have any vacancies?

Ja, ein Doppelzimmer.
yah. ine dop-pel-tsim-mer

Yes, a double room.

Haben Sie ein Kinderbett?
hah-ben zee ine kin-der-bet

Do you have a crib?

4 Words to remember

Familiarize yourself with these words and test yourself by concealing the German on the right with the cover flap.

air-conditioning	**die Klimaanlage** dee klee-mah-un-lah-ge
room	**das Zimmer** duss tsim-mer
single room	**das Einzelzimmer** duss ine-tsel-tsim-mer
double room	**das Doppelzimmer** duss dop-pel-tsim-mer
twin beds	**die zwei Einzelbetten** dee tsvie ine-tsel-bet-ten
bathroom	**das Badezimmer** duss bah-de-tsim-mer
shower	**die Dusche** dee doo-she
breakfast	**das Frühstück** duss frew-shtewk
key	**der Schlüssel** dair shlews-sel
balcony	**der Balkon** dair bull-kong

Hat das Zimmer Blick auf den Park?
hut duss tsim-mer blick owf dayn park
Does the room have a view over the park?

5 Say it

Do you have a single room, please?

Does the room have a balcony?

Cultural tip Some, but not all, hotels and guest houses will include breakfast in the price of a room; in others you will be charged extra. Often breakfast is in the style of a "Frühstücks-büffet" (breakfast buffet) and includes cereals, a selection of breads, cooked meats, cheeses, jams, fruit juices, and a choice of coffee or tea.

Wie lange möchten Sie bleiben?
vee lun-ge merkh-ten zee blie-ben
How long will you be staying?

Drei Nächte.
drie nekh-te

For three nights.

Sehr gut. Hier ist Ihr Schlüssel.
zair goot. heer isst eer shlews-sel

That's fine. Here's your key.

1 Warm up

How do you say "is there...?" and "there isn't..."? (pp.48–9)

What does "Haben Sie reserviert?" mean? (pp.20–1)

Im Hotel
In the hotel

Although rooms in larger hotels almost always have private bathrooms, there are still some **Pensionen** and guest houses where you will have to share facilities with other guests. Prices are generally charged for the room, and not per person, so a family staying in one room can be a cheap option.

2 Match and repeat

Match the numbered items in this hotel bedroom with the German text in the panel and test yourself using the cover flap.

1 **der Nachttisch**
dair nukht-tish

2 **die Lampe**
dee lum-pe

3 **die Musikanlage**
dee moo-zik-an-lah-ge

4 **die Vorhänge**
dee foer-hen-ge

5 **die Couch**
dee kowtch

6 **das Kopfkissen**
duss kopf-kis-sen

7 **das Kissen**
duss kis-sen

8 **das Bett**
duss bet

9 **die Tagesdecke**
dee tah-ges-dek-ke

10 **die Decke**
dee dek-ke

❶ *nightstand* ❹ *curtains*
❷ *lamp*
❸ *stereo system*
sofa ❺
❽ *bed*
blanket ❿
❻ *pillow* ❼ *cushion* ❾ *bedspread*

Cultural tip Hotel prices vary widely. They are higher during the season in summer or winter resorts. They are often much higher in cities during trade fairs and festivals, such as the Frankfurt Book Fair, the Berlinale Film Festival, the Cologne carnival, the Hanover computer fair (CEBIT), or the Munich October beer festival.

3 Useful phrases

Learn these phrases and then test yourself using the cover flap.

The room is too warm/cold.

Das Zimmer ist zu warm/kalt.
duss tsim-mer isst tsoo varm/kullt

There are no towels.

Es gibt keine Handtücher
es geept kie-ne hunt-tew-kher

I need some soap.

Ich brauche Seife.
ikh brow-khe zie-fe

The shower doesn't work.

Die Dusche funktioniert nicht.
dee doo-she foonk-tsee-oe-neert nikht

The elevator is broken.

Der Fahrstuhl ist kaputt.
dair fahr-shtool isst ka-poott

4 Put into practice

Cover the text on the right and complete the dialogue in German.

Kann ich Ihnen helfen?
kunn ikh eenen hel-fen
Can I help you?

Say: I need blankets.

Ich brauche Decken.
ikh brow-khe dek-ken

Das Zimmermädchen wird sie bringen.
duss tsim-mer-met-khen virt zee brin-gen
The maid will bring some.

Say: And the television is broken.

Und der Fernseher ist kaputt.
oont dair fairn-zay-er isst ka-poott

1 Warm up

Ask "Can I?" (pp.34–5)

What is German for "the shower"? (pp.58–9)

Say "I need some towels." (pp.60–1)

Beim Camping
Camping

Camping has long been popular in Germany. There are numerous campgrounds all over the country. These tend to be of a high standard, usually equipped with bathrooms, kitchens, shops, restaurants, and sometimes a swimming pool. Tourist offices have information about sites in their area.

2 Useful phrases

Learn these phrases. Then test yourself by concealing the German with the cover flap.

Kann ich ein Fahrrad ausleihen? kunn ikh ine fahr-raht ows-lie-en	*Can I rent a bicycle?*
Ist das Wasser trinkbar? isst duss vuss-ser trink-bahr	*Is this drinking water?*
Sind Lagerfeuer erlaubt? zint lah-ger-foy-er er-lowpt	*Are campfires allowed?*
Radios sind verboten. rah-dee-os zint fer-boe-ten	*Radios are not allowed.*

der Campingplatz ist ruhig.
dair kam-ping-pluts isst roo-hik
The campground is quiet.

das Campingplatz-büro
duss kamping-plutz-bew-roe
campsite office

das Überzelt
duss ew-ber-tselt
fly sheet

3 In conversation

Ich brauche einen Platz für zwei Tage.
ikh brow-khe ie-nen pluts fewr tsvie tah-ge

I need a site for two days.

Es gibt einen beim Schwimmbad.
es geept ie-nen bime shvim-bad

There's one near the swimming pool.

Wieviel kostet es für einen Wohnwagen?
vee-feel kos-tet es fewr ie-nen vohn-vah-gen

How much is it for a camper?

4 Words to remember

Familiarize yourself with these words and test yourself using the flap.

5 Say it

I need a site for four days.

Can I rent a tent?

Where's the electrical hookup?

tent	**das Zelt** duss tselt
camper trailer	**der Wohnwagen** dair voen-vah-gen
camper van	**das Wohnmobil** duss voen-moe-beel
campground	**der Campingplatz** dair kam-ping-pluts
site	**der Platz** dair pluts
campfire	**das Lagerfeuer** duss lah-ger-foy-er
drinking water	**das Trinkwasser** duss trink-vuss-ser
garbage	**der Abfall** dair up-full
showers	**die Duschen** dee doo-shen
stove fuel	**das Campinggas** duss kam-ping-gahs
sleeping bag	**der Schlafsack** dair shlahf-zuck
air mattress	**die Luftmatratze** dee looft-mah-trat-se
groundsheet	**der Zeltboden** dair tselt-bo-den

die Toiletten
dee twah-let-ten
restrooms

der Stromanschluss
dair shtrohm-un-shlooss
electrical hookup

die Zeltschnur
dee tselt-schnoor
guy rope

der Hering
dair hay-ring
tent peg

Fünfzig Euro, einen Tag im voraus.
fewnf-tsik oy-roe, ie-nen tahk im for-ows

Fifty euros, one day in advance.

Kann ich einen Grill mieten?
kunn ikh ie-nen grill mee-ten

Can I rent a barbecue?

Ja, aber sie müssen eine Kaution hinterlegen.
yah, ah-ber zee mews-sen ie-ne kow-tsee-oen hin-ter-lay-gen

Yes, but you must pay a deposit.

1 Warm up

How do you say "hot" and "cold"? (pp.60–1)

What is the German for "room," "bed," and "pillow"? (pp.60–1)

Beschreibungen
Descriptions

Simple descriptive sentences are easily constructed in German: **Das Zimmer ist kalt** (*the room is cold*). Note that when adjectives are put first, they may have different endings, such as **-er**, **-e**, **-es**, or **-en**—for example, **ein kaltes Zimmer** (*a cold room*). Just learn these in context as you encounter them.

2 Words to remember

Learn these words and then test yourself.

hart hart	*hard*
weich viekh	*soft*
heiß hiess	*hot*
kalt kullt	*cold*
groß groes	*big/tall*
klein kline	*small/short*
schön shern	*beautiful*
hässlich hess-likh	*ugly*
laut lowt	*noisy*
ruhig roo-hig	*quiet*
gut goot	*good*
schlecht shlekht	*bad*
langsam lung-zahm	*slow*
schnell shnell	*fast*
dunkel doon-kel	*dark*
hell hell	*light*

Die Berge sind hoch.
dee ber-ge zint hoekh
The mountains are high.

Der Hügel ist niedrig.
dair hew-gel isst nee-drikh
The hill is low.

Die Kirche ist alt.
dee kir-khe isst alt
The church is old.

Das Haus ist klein.
duss hows isst kline
The house is small.

Das Dorf ist sehr schön.
duss dorf isst zair shern
The village is very beautiful.

3 Useful phrases

To qualify a description add **sehr** (*very*) or **zu** (*too*) in front of the adjective, or surround it with **nicht ... genug** (*not ... enough*).

This coffee is cold.	**Dieser Kaffee ist kalt.** dee-zer kuf-fay isst kullt

My room is very noisy.	**Mein Zimmer ist sehr laut.** mine tsim-mer isst zair lowt

My car is too small.	**Mein Auto ist zu klein.** mine ow-to isst tsoo kline

The bed is not soft enough.	**Das Bett ist nicht weich genug.** das bet isst nikht viekh ge-nookh

4 Put into practice

Join in this conversation. Cover up the text on the right and complete the dialogue in German. Check and repeat if necessary.

Hier ist das Zimmer. heer isst duss tsim-mer *Here is the room.* *Say: The view is very beautiful.*	**Die Aussicht ist sehr schön.** dee ows-zikht isst zair shern

Dort ist das Badezimmer. dort isst duss bah-de-tsim-mer *There is the bathroom.* *Say: It is too small.*	**Es ist zu klein.** es isst tsoo kline

Wir haben sonst keins. veer hah-ben zonst keins *We don't have another one.* *Say: Then we'll take the room.*	**Dann nehmen wir das Zimmer.** dan nay-men veer duss tsim-mer

Wiederholung
Review and repeat

1 Adjectives

1 *The room is too hot.*

2 *My pillow is too small.*

3 *The coffee is good.*

4 *The bathroom is very cold.*

5 *My car is not big enough.*

1 Adjectives

What do these sentences mean?

1 Das Zimmer ist zu heiß.

2 Mein Kopfkissen ist zu klein.

3 Der Kaffee ist gut.

4 Das Badezimmer ist sehr kalt.

5 Mein Auto ist nicht groß genug.

2 Campground

1 **der Stromanschluss**
dair shtrohm-un-shlooss

2 **das Zelt**
duss tselt

3 **die Zeltschnur**
dee tselt-shnoor

4 **die Toiletten**
dee twah-let-ten

5 **der Wohnwagen**
dair voen-vah-gen

2 Campground

Name these items you might find in a campground.

1 *electrical hookup*

2 *tent*

3 *guy rope*

3 At the hotel

You are booking a room in a hotel. Follow the conversation, replying in German following the English prompts.

Kann ich Ihnen helfen?
1 *Do you have any vacancies?*

Ja, ein Doppelzimmer.
2 *Are pets allowed?*

Ja, wie lange möchten Sie bleiben?
3 *Three nights.*

Das macht zweihundertfünfzig Euro.
4 *Is breakfast included?*

Selbstverständlich, hier ist der Schlüssel.
5 *Thank you very much.*

3 At the hotel

1 **Haben Sie noch Zimmer frei?**
hah-ben zee nokh tsim-mer frie

2 **Sind Tiere zugelassen?**
zint tee-re tsoo-ge-luss-sen

3 **Drei Nächte.**
drie nekh-te

4 **Ist das Frühstück inbegriffen?**
isst duss frew-shtewk in-be-grif-fen

5 **Vielen Dank.**
fee-len dunk

❹ restrooms

❺ camper

4 Negatives

Make these sentences negative using the verb in brackets.

1 **Ich _____ Kinder. (haben)**

2 **Sie _____ morgen nach Hamburg. (fahren)**

3 **Er _____ Wein. (möchten)**

4 **Ich _____ Zucker in meinem Kaffee. (nehmen)**

5 **Die Aussicht _____ sehr schön. (sein)**

4 Negatives

1 **habe keine**
hah-be kie-ne

2 **fährt nicht**
fairt nikht

3 **möchte keinen**
merkh-te kie-nen

4 **nehme keinen**
nay-me kie-nen

5 **ist nicht**
isst nikht

Einkaufen
Shopping

1 Warm up

Ask "How do I get to
the station?"
(pp.50–1)

Say "Turn left at the
traffic lights," "Go
straight ahead," "The
station is across from
the café." (pp.50–1)

Although shopping centers on the
outskirts of the cities are increasingly
important in Germany, there are still
many smaller, traditional, specialized
shops. Excellent local markets exist in
large cities and small villages. Ask the
Verkehrsbüro (*tourist office*) when the
local market day is held.

2 Match and repeat

Match the shops numbered 1–9 below and right to the German in
the panel. Then test yourself using the cover flap.

1 **die Bäckerei**
dee bek-ke-rie

2 **die Konditorei**
dee kon-dee-to-rie

3 **das Zeitungskiosk**
duss tsie-toongs-
kee-osk

❶ *bakery*

❷ *pastry shop*

4 **die Fleischerei**
dee flie-she-rie

5 **das Feinkost-
geschäft**
duss fine-kost-ge-
sheft

6 **die Buchhandlung**
dee bookh-hund-
loong

❹ *butcher shop*

❺ *delicatessen*

7 **das Fischgeschäft**
duss fish-ge-sheft

8 **die Apotheke**
dee a-po-tay-ke

9 **die Bank**
dee bunk

❼ *fishmonger*

❽ *pharmacy*

Cultural tip A German "Apotheke" (pharmacy)
dispenses both prescription and over-the-counter
medicines. It also sells a small range of upmarket health
and beauty products. Everyday toiletries such as soap and
shampoo are more usually obtained from the "Drogerie,"
which is often a self-service supermarket. These stores
do not, however, sell medicines of any kind.

3 Words to remember

Familiarize yourself with these words and test yourself using the flap.

Der Blumenladen
dair bloo-men-lah-den
florist

antique dealer	**der Antiquitätenladen** dair an-ti-qvi-tay-ten-lah-den
hairdresser	**der Friseur** dair fri-zer
jeweler	**der Juwelier** dair yoo-ve-leer
post office	**die Post** dee posst
shoe shop	**das Schuhgeschäft** duss shoo-ge-sheft
dry-cleaner	**das Benzinbad** duss ben-tseen-baht
hardware store	**der Eisenwarenhändler** dair ie-zen-vah-ren-hend-ler

❸ *newsstand*

❻ *bookstore*

❾ *bank*

4 Useful phrases

Familiarize yourself with these phrases.

Where can I find the hairdresser?	**Wo ist der Friseur?** voe isst dair fri-zer
Where do I pay?	**Wo kann ich zahlen?** voe kunn ikh tsah-len
Thank you, I'm just looking.	**Danke, ich schaue mich nur um.** dun-ke, ikh show-e mikh noor oomm
Do you sell phone cards?	**Verkaufen Sie Telefonkarten?** fer-kow-fen zee tay-lay-foen-kar-ten
I'd like two of these.	**Ich hätte gern zwei von diesen.** ikh het-te gairn tsvie fon dee-zen
Is there a department store in town?	**Gibt es in der Stadt ein Kaufhaus?** geept es in dair shtutt ine kowf-hows
Can I place an order?	**Kann ich bitte bestellen?** kunn ikh bit-te be-shtel-len

5 Say it

Where can I find the bank?

Do you sell cheese?

Where do I pay?

Auf dem Markt
At the market

1 Warm up

What is German for 40, 56, 77, 82, and 94? (pp.30–1)

Say "I'd like a big room." (pp.64–5)

Ask "Do you have a small car?" (pp.64–5)

Germany uses the metric system of weights and measures. You need to ask for produce in kilograms or grams. You may find that the older generation still uses the term **ein Pfund** (*a pound*) meaning half a kilo. Larger items, such as melons, are sold **im Stück** (*individually*).

2 Match and repeat

Match the numbered items in this scene with the text in the panel.

1 **der Rhabarber**
  dair ra-bar-ber

2 **die Kartoffeln**
  dee kar-toff-eln

3 **die Radieschen**
  dee ra-dees-khen

4 **der Spinat**
  dair shpee-naht

5 **die Möhren**
  dee mer-ren

6 **der Kohl**
  dair koel

7 **die Lauche**
  dee low-khe

8 **der Kohlrabi**
  dair koel-rah-bee

rhubarb ❶ *potatoes* ❷ ❸ *radishes*

cabbage ❻ ❽ *kohlrabi* ❼ *leeks*

3 In conversation

Ich hätte gern Tomaten.
ikh het-te gairn to-mah-ten

I'd like some tomatoes.

Die großen oder die kleinen?
dee groe-sen oe-der dee klie-nen

The large ones or the small ones?

Zwei Kilo kleine, bitte.
tsvie kee-lo klie-ne, bit-te

Two kilos of the small ones, please.

> **█ Cultural tip** Germany uses the common
> European currency, the euro, divided into 100 cents.
> You will usually hear the price as "zehn Euro zwanzig"
> (€10.20). Often, the word "Euro" is also omitted:
> "zwei dreißig" (€2.30).

5 Say it

Three kilos of
potatoes, please.

The carrots are too
expensive.

How much is the
cabbage?

4 spinach

5 carrots

4 Useful phrases

In German you don't need a word for "of"
between the measurement unit (kilo) and
the thing you are buying: **ein Kilo Kirschen**
(*a kilo of cherries*).

**Diese Würstchen sind
zu teuer.**
dee-ze vewrst-khen zint
tsoo toy-er

*These sausages are too
expensive.*

**Was kostet ein Kilo
Trauben?**
vuss kos-tet ine kee-lo-
trowben

*How much is a kilo of
grapes?*

Das ist alles.
duss isst ull-les

That's all.

Sonst noch etwas?
zonst nokh et-vuss

Anything else?

**Das ist alles, danke.
Was kostet das?**
duss isst ull-les, dun-ke.
vuss kos-tet duss

*That's all, thank you.
How much?*

Drei Euro fünfzig.
drie oy-roe fewnf-tsik

Three euros, fifty.

What are these items you could buy in a supermarket?
(pp.24–5)

das Fleisch
der Fisch
der Käse
der Fruchtsaft
der Wein
das Wasser

Im Supermarkt
At the supermarket

Supermarkets in Germany range from the very well stocked at the expensive end of the market to much cheaper, budget chains. Some larger supermarkets, often in the basement of department stores, have small restaurants where you can sample the produce as you shop.

2 Match and repeat

Look at the numbered items and match them to the German words in the panel on the left. Then test yourself using the cover flap.

1 **die Haushalts-waren**
dee hows-hults-vah-ren

2 **das Obst**
duss opst

3 **die Getränke**
dee ge-tren-ke

4 **die Fertiggerichte**
dee fair-tikh-ge-rikh-te

5 **die Kosmetika**
dee kos-may-tee-ka

6 **die Milchprodukte**
dee milkh-pro-dook-te

7 **das Gemüse**
duss ge-mew-ze

8 **die Tiefkühlkost**
dee teef-kewl-kost

household products **1**

fruit **2**

drinks **3**

prepared meals **4**

vegetables **7**

frozen foods **8**

Cultural tip In Germany it is unusual and frowned upon to ask for a plastic bag for your purchases, and you will have to pay for them. Instead, people use their own baskets or reusable cotton bags that are sold at supermarkets.

3 Useful phrases

Learn these phrases and then test yourself using the cover flap.

May I have a bag?

Ich hätte gern eine Tragetasche.
ikh het-te gairn ie-ne trah-ge-tush-e

Where is the drinks aisle?

Wo ist der Gang mit den Getränken?
voe isst dair gung mit den ge-tren-ken

Where is the check-out, please?

Wo ist die Kasse, bitte?
voe isst dee kuss-se, bit-te

Please type in your PIN.

Bitte geben Sie Ihre Geheimzahl ein
bit-te gay-ben zee ee-re ge-hime-tsahl ine

4 Words to remember

Familiarize yourself with these words and then test yourself.

5 beauty products

6 dairy products

bread	**das Brot** duss broet
milk	**die Milch** dee milkh
butter	**die Butter** dee boott-ter
ham	**der Schinken** dair shin-ken
salt	**das Salz** duss zullts
pepper	**der Pfeffer** dair pfeff-fer
laundry detergent	**das Waschpulver** duss vush-pool-fer
toilet paper	**das Toilettenpapier** duss twah-let-ten-pa-peer
dishwashing liquid	**das Geschirrspülmittel** duss ge-sheerr-shpewl-mit-tel

5 Say it

Where's the dairy products aisle?

May I have some ham, please?

Where are the restrooms?

1 Warm up

Say "I'd like...".
(pp.22–3)

Ask "Do you have...?
(pp.12–13)

Say "38," "42," and
"46." (pp.30–1)

Say "big" and "small."
(pp.64–5)

Bekleidung und Schuhe
Clothes and shoes

When buying clothes, it is useful to know the colors. In German, colors can be adjectives or nouns; in the latter case they start with a capital: **Der Rock ist rot** (*The skirt is red*) but **Ich nehme das in Rot** (*I'll take this in red*).

2 Match and repeat

Match the numbered items of clothing to the German words in the panel on the left.

1 **das Hemd**
duss hemt

2 **die Krawatte**
dee kra-vutt-te

3 **die Jacke**
dee yuk-ke

4 **die Tasche**
dee ta-she

5 **der Ärmel**
dair airr-mel

6 **die Hose**
dee hoe-ze

7 **der Rock**
dair rok

8 **die Strumpfhose**
dee shtroompf-
hoe-ze

9 **die Schuhe**
dee shoo-e

shirt ❶

tie ❷

jacket ❸

pocket ❹

sleeve ❺

pants ❻

Cultural tip Like most of Europe, Germany uses the continental system of sizes. Dress sizes usually range from 36 (US 10) through to 46 (US 18) and shoe sizes from 37 (US 6) to 45 (US 12). For men's shirts, a size 41 is a 16-inch collar, 43 is a 17-inch collar, and 45 is an 18-inch collar.

3 Useful phrases

Learn these phrases and then test yourself using the cover flap.

I'll take this in pink.

Ich nehme das in Rosa.
ikh nay-me duss in ro-sa

Do you have this a size larger/smaller?

Haben Sie das eine Nummer größer/kleiner?
hah-ben zee duss ie-ne noom-mer grer-ser/klie-ner

It's not what I'm looking for.

Es ist nicht das, was ich suche.
es isst nikht duss, vuss ikh zoo-khe

4 Words to remember

Familiarize yourself with these words and test yourself using the cover flap.

red	**rot**	roet
white	**weiß**	vies
blue	**blau**	blow
yellow	**gelb**	gelp
green	**grün**	grewn
black	**schwarz**	shvarts

❼ *skirt*

❽ *pantyhose*

❾ *shoes*

5 Say it

Do you have this jacket in black?

Do you have this in a 38?

Do you have a size smaller?

Wiederholung
Review and repeat

1 Market

1 **die Kartoffeln**
dee kar-toff-eln

2 **die Radieschen**
dee ra-dees-khen

3 **der Spinat**
dair shpee-naht

4 **der Kohl**
dair koel

5 **der Lauch**
dair lowkh

6 **die Möhren**
dee mer-ren

1 Market

Name the numbered items. Conceal the answers with the cover flap, then check that you have remembered the German correctly.

1 *potatoes*
2 *radishes*
3 *spinach*
4 *cabbage*
5 *leeks*
6 *carrots*

2 Description

1 *These shoes are too expensive.*

2 *My room is very small.*

3 *The bed is too hard.*

2 Description

What do these sentences mean?

1 **Diese Schuhe sind zu teuer.**

2 **Mein Zimmer ist sehr klein.**

3 **Das Bett ist zu hart.**

3 Shops

1 **die Bäckerei**
dee bek-ke-rie

2 **die Bank**
dee bunk

3 **die Buchhandlung**
dee bookh-hund-loong

4 **das Fischgeschäft**
duss fish-ge-sheft

5 **die Konditorei**
dee kon-dee-to-rie

6 **die Fleischerei**
dee flie-she-rie

3 Shops

Name the numbered shops in German. Then check your answers.

1 *bakery*
2 *bank*
3 *bookstore*

4 *fishmonger*
5 *pastry shop*
6 *butcher shop*

4 Supermarket

Name the numbered items. Cover the answers with the flap and then check to see if you remembered correctly.

❶ household products

❷ beauty products

❸ drinks

❹ dairy products

❺ vegetables

4 Supermarket

1 **die Haushalts-waren**
dee hows-hults-vah-ren

2 **die Kosmetika**
dee kos-may-tee-ka

3 **die Getränke**
dee ge-tren-ke

4 **die Milchprodukte**
dee milkh-pro-dook-te

5 **das Gemüse**
duss ge-mew-ze

5 Museum

Follow this conversation replying in German following the English prompts.

Guten Tag. Kann ich Ihnen helfen?
1 *I'd like five tickets.*

Das macht siebzig Euro.
2 *That's very expensive!*

Wir geben keine Ermäßigung für Kinder.
3 *How much is a guide?*

Fünfzehn Euro.
4 *Five tickets and a guide, please.*

Fünfundachtzig Euro, bitte.
5 *Here you are. Where are the restrooms?*

Dort drüben.
6 *Thank you very much.*

5 Museum

1 **Ich hätte gern fünf Eintrittskarten.**
ikh het-te gairn fewnf ine-trits-kar-ten

2 **Das ist sehr teuer!**
duss isst zair toy-er

3 **Was kostet der Führer?**
vuss kos-tet dair few-rer

4 **Fünf Eintrittskarten und einen Führer, bitte.**
fewnf ine-trits-kar-ten oont ie-nen few-rer, bit-te

5 **Bitte sehr. Wo sind die Toiletten?**
bit-te zair. voe zint dee twah-let-ten

6 **Vielen Dank.**
fee-len dunk

1 Warm up

Ask "Which platform?" (pp.38–9)

What is the German for the following family members: sister, brother, mother, father, son, and daughter? (pp.10–11)

Berufe
Jobs

Most job titles are masculine. They can be turned into the feminine equivalent by adding **-in**: for example, **der Lehrer/die Lehrerin** (*male/female teacher*). You don't need to use the indefinite article "a" when you describe your job: **Ich bin Buchhalter** (*I'm an accountant*).

2 Words to remember: jobs

The feminine ending is shown in brackets. Some jobs change the main vowel to an umlaut for the feminine form: **Arzt/Ärztin** (*male/female doctor*).

Arzt/Ärztin artst/airts-tin	*doctor*
Zahnarzt/ Zahnärztin tsahn-artst/tsahn-airts-tin	*dentist*
Krankenpfleger/ Krankenschwester krunk-en-pflay-ger/ krunk-en-shves-ter	*nurse*
Lehrer(in) lay-rer(in)	*teacher*
Buchhalter(in) bookh-hull-ter(in)	*accountant*
Rechtsanwalt/ Rechtsanwältin rekhts-un-vullt/ rekhts-un-vel-tin	*lawyer*
Grafiker(in) grah-fi-ker(in)	*designer*
Berater(in) be-rah-ter(in)	*consultant*
Sekretär(in) zek-re-tair(in)	*secretary*
Verkäufer(in) fer-koy-fer(in)	*store clerk*
Elektriker(in) ay-lek-tree-ker(in)	*electrician*
Klempner(in) klemp-ner(in)	*plumber*
selbstständig zelpst-shten-dikh	*self-employed*

Ich bin Klempner.
ikh bin klemp-ner
I'm a plumber.

Sie ist Lehrerin.
zee isst lay-re-rin
She's a teacher.

3 Put into practice

Practice these phrases. Then cover up the text on the right and complete the dialogue in German.

Was machen Sie beruflich?
vuss ma-khen zee be-roof-likh
What do you do?

Say: I am a consultant.

Ich bin Berater.
ikh bin be-rah-ter

Bei welcher Firma arbeiten Sie?
bie vel-kher fir-ma ar-bie-ten zee
What company do you work for?

Say: I'm self-employed.

Ich bin selbstständig.
ikh bin zelpst-shten-dikh

Wie interessant!
vee in-tay-res-sunt
How interesting!

Ask: And what do you do?

Und was machen Sie beruflich?
oont vuss ma-khen zee be-roof-likh

Ich bin Zahnarzt.
ikh bin tsahn-artst
I'm a dentist.

Say: My sister is a dentist, too.

Mein Schwester ist auch Zahnärztin.
mie-ne shves-ter isst owkh tsahn-airts-tin

4 Words to remember: workplace

Familiarize yourself with these words and test yourself.

headquarters	**die Zentrale** dee tsen-trah-le
branch	**die Zweigstelle** dee tsviek-shtel-le
department	**die Abteilung** dee up-tie-loong
superior	**der/die Vorgesetzte** dair/dee for-ge-zets-te
trainee	**der Auszubildende** dair ows-tsoo-bilden-de
reception	**der Empfang** dair emp-fung

Die Zentrale ist in Bremen.
dee tsen-trah-le isst in bray-men
Headquarters is in Bremen.

1 Warm up

Practice different ways of introducing yourself in different situations. Mention your name, your occupation, and any other information you'd like to give. (pp.8–9, pp.14–15, and pp.78–9)

Das Büro
The office

In all countries, each company has its own special terms, but there are many items that are universal, and the English word is often used. Note that the German keyboard has a different layout from the standard "QWERTY" convention, and that **das Handy** is a cell phone.

2 Words to remember

Familiarize yourself with these words. Read them aloud several times and try to memorize them. Conceal the German with the cover flap and test yourself.

German	English
der Monitor dair mo-nee-tor	*monitor*
der Computer dair kom-pyoo-ter	*computer*
die Maus dee mows	*mouse*
die E-Mail dee ee-mayle	*email*
das Internet duss in-ter-net	*Internet*
das Passwort duss puss-vort	*password*
die Voice-Mail dee voyse-mayle	*voicemail*
das Fax duss fux	*fax machine*
der Fotokopierer dair fo-to-ko-pee-rer	*photocopier*
der Terminkalender dair terr-meen-ka-len-der	*planner*
die Visitenkarte dee vi-see-ten-kar-te	*business card*
die Besprechung dee be-shpre-khoong	*meeting*
die Konferenz dee kon-fay-rents	*conference*
die Tagesordnung dee tah-ges-ort-noong	*agenda*

❶ lamp

screen ❹

❷ stapler

telephone ❸

pen ❿

notepad ⓫

drawer ⓬

3 Useful phrases

Learn these phrases and then test yourself using the cover flap.

I need to photocopy something.

Ich muss etwas fotokopieren.
ikh mooss et-vuss fo-to-ko-pee-ren

I'd like to arrange an appointment.

Ich möchte einen Termin ausmachen.
ikh merkh-te ie-nen tair-meen ows-ma-khen

I want to send an email.

Ich möchte eine E-Mail schicken.
ikh merkh-te ie-ne ee-mayle shik-ken

4 Match and repeat

Match the numbered items to the words in the panel and test yourself.

5 *keyboard*

6 *laptop*

printer **9**

7 *desk*

8 *clock*

13 *swivel chair*

1 **die Lampe**
dee lum-pe

2 **das Heftgerät**
duss heft-ge-rayt

3 **das Telefon**
duss tay-lay-foen

4 **der Bildschirm**
dair bilt-sheerm

5 **die Tastatur**
dee tuss-tah-toor

6 **der Laptop**
dair lap-top

7 **der Schreibtisch**
dair shriep-tish

8 **die Uhr**
dee oor

9 **der Drucker**
dair drook-ker

10 **der Stift**
dair shtift

11 **der Notizblock**
dair no-teets-blok

12 **die Schublade**
dee shoop-lah-de

13 **der Drehstuhl**
dair dray-shtool

5 Say it

I'd like to arrange a conference.

I need to send a fax.

Do you have a laptop?

Say "How interesting!"
(pp.78–9) and
"library." (pp.48–9)

Ask "What do you
do?" and answer "I'm
an accountant."
(pp.78–9)

Die Akademische Welt
Academic world

At German universities, you have to earn credits, often over many years, before you can take the final exam. The first degree is either a **Staatsexamen** (*state exam*) or a **Magister** (*MA*), which can be followed by a **Doktorat** (*PhD*).

2 Useful phrases

Learn these phrases and then test yourself using the cover flap.

Was ist Ihr Gebiet? vuss isst eer ge-beet	*What is your field?*	
Ich betreibe Forschungen in Biochemie. ikh be-trie-be for-shoong-en in bee-oe-khay-mee	*I am doing research in biochemistry.*	
Ich habe Jura studiert. ikh hah-be yoo-ra shtoo-deert	*I studied law.*	
Ich halte einen Vortrag über moderne Architektur. ikh hul-te ie-nen vor-trahk ew-ber mo-dair-ne ar-khi-tek-toor	*I am giving a presentation on modern architecture.*	

3 In conversation

Guten Tag, ich bin Professor Stein.
goo-ten tahk, ikh bin pro-fes-sor shtien

Hello, I'm Professor Stein.

An welcher Universität arbeiten Sie?
un vel-kher oo-nee-vair-zee-tayt ar-bie-ten zee

What university do you work at?

Ich bin Delegierte der Humboldt-Universität.
ikh bin day-lay-ge-ter dair hoomm-bolt-oo-nee-vair-zee-tayt

I'm the delegate from Humboldt University.

4 Words to remember

Familiarize yourself with these words and then test yourself.

conference	**die Konferenz**	dee kon-fay-rents
trade fair	**die Handelsmesse**	dee hun-dels-mes-se
seminar	**das Seminar**	duss zay-mee-nahr
lecture hall	**der Vorlesungssaal**	dair for-lay-zoongs-zahl
conference room	**das Konferenzzimmer**	duss kon-fay-rents-tsim-mer
exhibition	**die Ausstellung**	dee ows-shtel-loong
assistant professor	**der Dozent(in)**	dair do-tsent(in)
professor	**der Professor(in)**	dair pro-fes-sor(in)
medicine	**die Medizin**	dee may-dee-tseen
science	**die Naturwissenschaften**	dee na-toor-vis-sen-shuff-ten
humanities	**die Geisteswissen-schaften**	dee gies-tes-vis-sen-shuff-ten
engineering	**die Technik**	dee tekh-nik

Wir haben einen Stand.
veer hah-ben ie-nen shtunt
We have a stand.

5 Say it

I'm doing research in medicine.

I studied humanities.

She's the professor.

Was ist Ihr Gebiet?
vuss isst eer ge-beet

What's your field?

Ich betreibe Forschungen in Technik.
ikh be-trie-be for-shoong-en in tekh-nik

I'm doing research in engineering.

Wie interessant!
vee in-tay-res-sunt

How interesting!

1 Warm up

Ask "Can I ...?"
(pp.34–5)

Say "I want to send an
email." (pp.80–1)

Ask "Can you send a
fax?" (pp.80–1)

Geschäftliches
In business

You will receive a more friendly
reception and make a good impression
if you make the effort to begin a
meeting with a short introduction in
German, even if your vocabulary is
limited. After that, all parties will
probably be happy to continue the
meeting in English.

2 Words to remember

Familiarize yourself with these words and
then test yourself by concealing the
German with the cover flap.

der Kunde
dair koonn-de
client

der Zeitplan dair tsiet-plahn	*schedule*
die Lieferung dee lee-fe-roong	*delivery*
die Bezahlung dee be-tsah-loong	*payment*
das Budget duss bew-jay	*budget*
der Preis dair priez	*price*
die Akte dee ukk-te	*document*
die Rechnung dee rekh-noong	*invoice*
die Zahlen dee tsah-len	*figures*
der Kostenvoranschlag dair kos-ten-for-un-shlahk	*estimate*
der Gewinn dair ge-vinn	*profits*
der Absatz dair up-zuts	*sales*

Cultural tip Many German companies
have "Gleitzeit," flexible working hours. Generally,
offices start at 9 am or before, break for lunch at
12 noon, and finish at about 5 pm or earlier. In larger
firms and offices, lunch is often eaten in a subsidized
cafeteria together with colleagues.

3 Useful phrases

Familiarize yourself with these phrases and then test yourself using the cover flap to conceal the German.

Sollen wir den Vertrag unterzeichnen?
zol-len veer dayn fer-trahk oon-ter-tsiekh-nen
Shall we sign the contract?

die Managerin
dee man-a-je-rin
executive

der Vertrag
dair fer-trahk
contract

Bitte schicken Sie mir den Vertrag.
bit-te shik-ken zee meer dayn fer-trahk

Please send me the contract.

Haben wir uns auf einen Zeitplan geeinigt?
hah-ben veer oons owf ie-nen tsiet-plahn ge-ie-nikht

Have we agreed on a schedule?

Wann können Sie liefern?
vunn kern-nen zee lee-fairn

When can you deliver?

Was ist das Budget?
vuss isst duss bew-jay

What's the budget?

Können Sie mir die Rechnung schicken?
kern-nen zee meer dee rekh-noong shik-ken

Can you send me the invoice?

der Bericht
dair be-rikht
report

4 Say it

Can you send me the estimate?

Have we agreed on a price?

What are the profits?

Wiederholung
Review and repeat

Antworten
Answers
Cover with flap

1 At the office

1 **das Heftgerät**
duss heft-ge-rayt

2 **die Lampe**
dee lum-pe

3 **der Laptop**
dair lap-top

4 **der Stift**
dair shtift

5 **der Schreibtisch**
dair shriep-tish

6 **der Notizblock**
dair no-teets-blok

7 **die Uhr**
dee oor

1 At the office

Name these items.

2 *lamp*

laptop **3**

4 *pen*

1 *stapler*

5 *desk*   *notepad* **6**

2 Jobs

1 **Arzt/Ärztin**
artst/airts-tin

2 **Klempner(in)**
klemp-ner(in)

3 **Verkäufer(in)**
fer-koy-fer(in)

4 **Buchhalter(in)**
bookh-hull-ter(in)

5 **Lehrer(in)**
lay-rer(in)

6 **Rechtsanwalt/
Rechtsanwältin**
rekhts-un-vullt/
rekhts-un-vel-tin

2 Jobs

What are these jobs in German?

1 *doctor*

2 *plumber*

3 *store clerk*

4 *accountant*

5 *teacher*

6 *lawyer*

WORK AND STUDY **8 7**

Antworten
Answers
Cover with flap

clock **7**

3 Work

Answer these questions following the English prompts.

Bei welcher Firma arbeiten Sie?
1 *Say: I work for myself.*

Von welcher Universität sind Sie?
2 *Say: I'm at the University of Köln.*

Was ist Ihr Gebiet?
3 *Say: I'm doing medical research.*

Haben wir uns auf einen Zeitplan geeinigt?
4 *Say: Yes, my secretary has the schedule.*

3 Work

1 **Ich bin selbstständig.**
ikh bin zelpst-shten-dikh

2 **Ich bin von der Universität Köln.**
ikh bin fon dair oo-nee-vair-zee-tayt kewln

3 **Ich betreibe Forschungen in der Medizin.**
ikh be-trie-be for-shoong-en in dair may-dee-tseen

4 **Ja, meine Sekretärin hat den Zeitplan.**
yah, mye-ne zek-re-tair-in hut dayn tsiet-plahn

4 How much?

Answer the question with the amount shown in brackets.

1 **Was kostet der Kaffee?** (€2.50)

2 **Was kostet das Zimmer?** (€47)

3 **Was kostet das Kilo Tomaten?** (€3.25)

4 **Was kostet der Parkplatz für drei Tage?** (€50)

4 How much?

1 **Das macht zwei Euro fünfzig.**
duss makht tsvie oy-roe fewnf-tsik

2 **Es kostet siebenundvierzig Euro.**
es kos-tet zee-ben-oont-feer-tsik oy-roe

3 **Das macht drei Euro fünfundzwanzig.**
duss makht drie oy-roe fewnf-oont-tsvun-tsik

4 **Er kostet fünfzig Euro.**
air kos-tet fewnf-tsik oy-roe

In der Apotheke
At the pharmacy

German pharmacies are indicated by a stylized red letter "A" for **Apotheke**. Pharmacists dispense a wide variety of medicines over the counter. They advise and can even give injections, if necessary. In larger towns, a duty roster ensures that there is always one pharmacy that is open.

2 Match and repeat

Match the numbered items to the German words in the panel on the left and test yourself using the cover flap.

1 **der Verband**
dair fer-bunt

2 **der Sirup**
dair zee-roop

3 **die Tropfen**
dee trop-fen

4 **das Pflaster**
duss pflus-ter

5 **die Spritze**
dee shprit-se

6 **die Salbe**
dee zull-be

7 **das Zäpfchen**
duss tsepf-khen

8 **die Tablette**
dee tub-let-te

bandage ❶ *syrup* ❷

drops ❸

❹ *adhesive bandage* *syringe* ❺

3 In conversation

Guten Tag, Sie wünschen.
goo-ten tahk, zee vewn-shen

Hello. What would you like?

Ich habe Bauchschmerzen.
ikh hah-be bowkh-shmairt-sen

I have a stomachache.

Haben Sie Durchfall?
hah-ben zee doorkh-full

Do you have diarrhea?

4 Words to remember

In German you don't use the indefinite article "a" to describe a pain.

Ich habe Kopfschmerzen.
ikh hah-be
kopf-shmairt-sen
I have a headache.

headache	**Kopfschmerzen**	kopf-shmairt-sen
stomachache	**Bauchschmerzen**	bowkh-shmairt-sen
diarrhea	**Durchfall**	doorkh-full
cold (in the nose)	**der Schnupfen**	dair shnoop-fen
cough	**der Husten**	dair hoos-ten
sunburn	**der Sonnenbrand**	dair zon-nen-brunt
toothache	**Zahnschmerzen**	tsahn-shmairt-sen

6 Say it

I have a cold.

Do you have that as an ointment?

Do you have a cough?

6 ointment

7 suppository

8 tablet

5 Useful phrases

Learn these phrases and then test yourself using the cover flap.

I have a sunburn.	**Ich haben einen Sonnenbrand.** ikh hah-be ie-nen zon-nen-brunt
Do you have that as a syrup?	**Haben Sie das auch als Sirup?** hah-ben zee duss owkh ulls zee-roop
I'm allergic to penicillin.	**Ich bin allergisch gegen Penizillin.** ikh bin ull-lair-gish gay-gen pay-nee-tsee-leen

Nein, aber ich habe auch Kopfschmerzen.
nine, ah-ber ikh hah-be owkh kopf-shmairt-sen

No, but I also have a headache.

Nehmen Sie dies.
nay-men zee dees

Take this.

Haben Sie das auch als Tabletten?
hah-ben zee duss owkh ulls tub-let-ten

Do you have that as tablets?

Der Körper
The body

In German many health-related expressions are reflexive—that is, the equivalent of "I am not feeling well" in German is **Ich fühle mich nicht wohl** (literally, *I am not feeling myself well*). As in English, the reflexive pronoun (myself, yourself, etc.) changes, depending on the context.

2 Match and repeat

Match the numbered parts of the body with the list on the left.

1 **die Hand**
   dee hunt

2 **der Kopf**
   dair kopf

3 **die Schulter**
   dee shool-ter

4 **der Ellbogen**
   dair el-bo-gen

5 **das Haar, die Haare**
   duss hahr, dee hah-re

6 **der Arm**
   dair arm

7 **der Hals**
   dair hulls

8 **die Brust**
   dee broost

9 **der Bauch**
   dair bowkh

10 **das Bein**
   duss bine

11 **das Knie**
   duss k-nee

12 **der Fuß**
   dair fooss

hand **1**
head **2**
shoulder **3**
4 *elbow*
5 *hair*
6 *arm*
7 *neck*
8 *chest*
9 *stomach*
10 *leg*
11 *knee*
12 *foot*

3 Match and repeat

Match the numbered facial features with the list on the right.

eyebrow **1**

nose **3**

2 *eye*

4 *mouth*

ear **5**

1	**die Augenbraue** dee ow-gen-brow-e
2	**das Auge** duss ow-ge
3	**die Nase** dee nah-ze
4	**der Mund** dair moont
5	**das Ohr** duss ohr

4 Useful phrases

Learn these phrases and then test yourself using the cover flap.

I have a pain in my back.

Ich habe Schmerzen im Rücken.
ikh hah-be shmairt-sen im rewk-ken

I have a rash on my arm.

Ich habe einen Ausschlag am Arm.
ikh hah-be ie-nen ows-shluk um arm

I don't feel well.

Ich fühle mich nicht wohl.
ikh few-le mikh nikht voel

5 Put into practice

Join in this conversation and test yourself using the cover flap.

Was ist denn los?
vuss isst denn loes
What's the matter?

Say: *I'm not feeling well.*

Ich fühle mich nicht wohl.
ikh few-le mikh nikht voel

Wo tut es denn weh?
voe toot es den vayh
Where does it hurt?

Say: *I have a pain in my shoulder.*

Ich haben Schmerzen in der Schulter.
ikh hah-be shmairt-sen in dair shool-ter

1 Warm up

Say "I need some tablets" and "He needs some ointment." (pp.60–1 and pp.88–9)

What is the German for "I don't have a son"? (pp.10–15)

Beim Arzt
At the doctor

German doctors are titled according to their specialist qualifications, such as **Internist** (*internal medicine*) and **Kardiologe** (*heart specialist*). A general practitioner is known as **praktischer Arzt**. In most cases you'll need an appointment, or you can visit the hospital outpatient department.

2 Useful phrases you may hear

Learn these phrases and then test yourself using the cover flap to conceal the German.

Es ist nichts Ernsthaftes. es isst nikhts airnst-huff-tes	*It's not serious.*
Wir müssen ein paar Tests machen. veer mews-sen ine pahr tests ma-khen	*We need to do a few tests.*
Sie haben eine Niereninfektion. zee hah-ben ie-ne nee-ren-infek-tsee-oen	*You have an infection in your kidney.*
Sie müssen ins Krankenhaus gehen. zee mews-sen ins krunk-en-hows gay-en	*You need to go to the hospital.*

Nehmen Sie irgendwelche Medikamente?
nay-men zee ir-gent-vel-khe may-dee-ka-men-te
Are you taking any medication?

3 In conversation

Was ist denn los?
vuss isst den loes

What's the matter?

Ich habe Schmerzen in der Brust.
ikh hah-be shmairt-sen in dair broost

I have a pain in my chest.

Ich werde Sie untersuchen.
ikh vair-de zee oon-ter-zoo-khen

I'll examine you.

Cultural tip Before you go to Germany, find out if your health insurance covers emergency medical care in Europe; if it doesn't, purchase a travel medical insurance policy.

4 Useful phrases you may need to say

Learn these phrases and then test yourself using the cover flap.

I am diabetic.	**Ich bin Diabetiker(in).** ikh bin dee-ar-bay-ti-kair(in)
I am epileptic.	**Ich bin Epileptiker(in).** ikh bin ay-pee-lep-ti-kair(in)
I have asthma.	**Ich habe Asthma.** ikh hah-be ast-ma
I have a heart condition.	**Ich bin herzkrank.** ikh bin hairts-krunk
I have a fever.	**Ich habe Fieber.** ikh hah-be fee-ber
It's urgent.	**Es ist dringend.** es isst dring-ent
I feel faint.	**Ich fühle mich schwach.** ikh few-le mikh shvakh
I feel sick.	**Mir ist schlecht.** meer isst shlekht

Ich bin schwanger.
ikh bin shvun-ger
I'm pregnant.

5 Say it

It's serious.

My son needs to go to the hospital.

It's not urgent.

Ist es etwas Ernsthaftes?
isst es et-vuss airnst-huff-tes

Is it serious?

Nein, nur Verdauungs-beschwerden.
nine, noor fer-dow-oongs-be-shvair-den

No, only indigestion.

Ein Glück!
ine glewkk

What a relief!

1 Warm up

Say "how long" as in "how long is the trip?" (pp.42–3)

Ask "Do I need tests?" (pp.92–3)

Say "mouth" and "head." (pp.90–1)

Im Krankenhaus
At the hospital

It is useful to know a few basic phrases relating to hospitals for use in an emergency or in case you need to visit a friend or colleague in hospital. A ward in hospital is known as **die Station** and the equivalent of the outpatient department is known as **die Ambulanz**.

2 Useful phrases

Familiarize yourself with these phrases. Conceal the German with the cover flap and test yourself.

Wann ist Besuchszeit? vunn isst be-zookhs-tsiet	*What are the visiting hours?*
Wie lange wird das dauern? vee lun-ge virt duss dow-ern	*How long will it take?*
Tut das weh? toot duss vayh	*Will it hurt?*
Bitte legen Sie sich hier hin. bit-te lay-gen zee zikh heer hin	*Please lie down here.*
Sie dürfen nichts essen, zee dewr-fen nikhts es-sen	*You must not eat.*
Bewegen Sie nicht den Kopf. be-vay-gen zee nikht dayn kopf	*Don't move your head.*
Bitte öffnen Sie Ihren Mund. bit-te erf-nen zee ee-ren moont	*Please open your mouth.*
Wir müssen eine Blutprobe machen. veer mews-sen ie-ne bloot-proe-be ma-khen	*We'll have to do a blood test.*

die intravenöse Infusion
dee in-tra-vay-ner-ze in-foo-zee-oen
intravenous drip

Geht es Ihnen besser?
gayt es ee-nen bes-ser
Are you feeling better?

Wo ist das Wartezimmer?
voe isst duss var-te-tsim-mer
Where is the waiting room?

3 Words to remember

Memorize these words and test yourself using the cover flap.

emergency room	**die Unfallstation** dee oon-full-shtah-tsee-oen
X-ray department	**die Röntgenabteilung** dee rernt-gen-up-tie-loong
children's ward	**die Kinderstation** dee kin-der-shtah-tsee-oen
operating room	**der Operationssaal (der OP)** dair o-pay-rah-tsee-oens-zahl (dair oe-pay)
hall	**der Gang** dair gung
stairs	**die Treppe** dee trep-pe

Ire Rötgenaufhahme ist normal.
ee-re rernt-gen-owf-nah-me isst nor-mal
Your X-ray is normal.

4 Put into practice

Join in this conversation. Read the German on the left and follow the instructions to make your reply. Then test yourself by concealing the answers with the cover flap.

Sie haben eine Entzündung.
zee hah-ben ie-ne ent-tsewn-doong
You have an infection.

Ask: Will you need to do tests?

Müssen Sie Untersuchungen machen?
mews-sen zee oon-ter-zoo-khoong-en ma-khen

Zuerst machen wir eine Blutprobe.
tsoo-airst ma-khen veer ie-ne bloot-proe-be
First we will do a blood test.

Ask: Will it hurt?

Tut das weh?
toot duss vayh

5 Say it

Will you need to do a blood test?

Where is the children's ward?

Nein, keine Angst.
nine, kie-ne unkst
No. Don't worry.

Ask: How long will it take?

Wie lange wird das dauern?
vee lun-ge virt duss dow-ern

Wiederholung
Review and repeat

Antworten
Answers
Cover with flap

1 The body

1 **der Kopf**
dair kopf

2 **der Arm**
dair arm

3 **die Brust**
dee broost

4 **der Bauch**
dair bowkh

5 **das Bein**
duss bine

6 **das Knie**
duss k-nee

7 **der Fuß**
dair fooss

1 The body

Name the numbered body parts in German.

1 *head*

2 *arm*

chest **3**

4 *stomach*

leg **5**

6 *knee*

foot **7**

2 On the phone

1 **Ich möchte bitte Venny Gerlach sprechen.**
ikh merkh-te bit-te ven-nee gair-lakh shpre-khen

2 **Horst Richter von der Druckerei Gohl.**
horst rikh-ter fon dair drook-er-ie goel

3 **Kann ich eine Nachricht hinterlassen?**
kunn ikh ie-ne nahkh-rikht hin-ter-luss-sen

4 **Der Termin für Montag elf Uhr ist in Ordnung.**
dair terr-meen fewr mohn-tahk elf oor isst in ord-noong

2 On the phone

You are confirming an appointment with a business contact on the telephone. Join in the conversation, replying in German following the English prompts.

Hello, Firma Apex.
1 *I'd like to speak to Venny Gerlach.*

Ja, mit wem spreche ich?
2 *Horst Richter of Gohl Printers.*

Es tut mir Leid, da ist besetzt.
3 *Can I leave a message?*

Aber selbstverständlich.
4 *The appointment on Monday at 11 am is fine.*

3 Clothing

Say the German words for the numbered items of clothing.

tie ❶

jacket ❷

pants ❸

❹ *skirt*

shoes ❺

pantyhose ❻

3 Clothing

1 **die Krawatte**
dee kra-vutt-te

2 **die Jacke**
dee yuk-ke

3 **die Hose**
dee hoe-ze

4 **der Rock**
dair rok

5 **die Schuhe**
dee shoo-e

6 **die Strumpfhose**
dee shtroompf-
hoe-ze

4 At the doctor's

Say these phrases in German.

1 *I don't feel well.*

2 *Will you need to do tests?*

3 *I have a heart condition.*

4 *Do I need to go to the hospital?*

5 *I'm pregnant.*

4 At the doctor's

1 **Ich fühle mich nicht wohl.**
ikh fewh-le mikh nikht voel

2 **Müssen Sie Untersuchungen machen?**
mews-sen zee oon-ter-zoo-khoong-en ma-khen

3 **Ich bin herzkrank.**
ikh bin hairts-krunk

4 **Muss ich ins Krankenhaus gehen?**
mooss ikh ins krunk-en-hows gay-en

5 **Ich bin schwanger.**
ikh bin shvun-ger

1 Warm up

Say the months of
the year in German.
(pp.28–9)

Ask "Is there...?"
(pp.48–9)

Zu Hause
At home

Most Germans live in rented apartments (**die Wohnung**); relatively few
own their homes (**das Eigenheim**).
The size of a dwelling is given in
square meters and described in terms
of the number of rooms in addition to
kitchen and bathroom: 2 ZKB means
2 Zimmer, Küche, Badezimmer.

2 Match and repeat

Match the numbered items to the list and test yourself using the flap.

1 **das Dach**
duss dukh

2 **der Schornstein**
dair shorn-shtine

3 **die Dachrinne**
dee dukh-rin-ne

4 **der Blumenkasten**
dair bloo-men-
kass-ten

5 **die Mauer**
dee mow-er

6 **das Fenster**
duss fens-ter

7 **die Tür**
dee tewr

8 **Die Straße**
dee shtrah-se

chimney ②

roof ❶

⑤ *wall*   ⑥ *window*   *door* ❼

Conversational tip The German word
for a single-family dwelling is "Einfamilienhaus"
(one-family house). A duplex is called a
"Zweifamilienhaus" (two-family house), while a row
house is called a "Reihenhaus" (house in a row). The
downtown area of a city or town is the "Innenstadt,"
and a suburb is a "Vorstadt" or "Vorort."

3 Words to remember

Familiarize yourself with these words and test yourself using the flap.

Wie hoch ist die monatliche Miete?
vee hoekh isst dee mo-naht-li-khe mee-te
What is the rent per month?

room	**das Zimmer** duss tsim-mer	
floor	**der Fußboden** dair foos-bo-den	
ceiling	**die Decke** dee dek-ke	
bedroom	**das Schlafzimmer** duss shlahf-tsim-mer	
bathroom	**das Badezimmer** duss bah-de-tsim-mer	
kitchen	**die Küche** dee kew-khe	
dining room	**das Esszimmer** duss ess-tsim-mer	
living room	**das Wohnzimmer** duss vohn-tsim-mer	
basement	**der Keller** dair kel-ler	
attic	**der Dachboden** dair dukh-boe-den	

3 *gutter*

4 *window box*

8 *street*

4 Useful phrases

Learn these phrases and test yourself.

Gibt es eine Garage?
geept es ie-ne ga-ra-je

Is there a garage?

MAY MAI MAI MEI

Ab wann ist es frei?
up vunn isst es frie

When is it available?

Ist es möbliert?
isst es mer-bleert

Is it furnished?

5 Say it

Is there a dining room?

Is it large?

Is it available in July?

Is it furnished?

Im Haus
In the house

If you're renting an apartment or a
house in Germany, the rent is often
described as **kalt** (*cold*). This means
that services such as electricity have to
be paid for in addition to the basic
rent; be sure to check this in advance.
Furnished apartments in vacation
resorts are known as **Ferienwohnung**.

2 Match and repeat

Match the numbered items to the list in the
panel on the left. Then test yourself by
concealing the German with the cover flap.

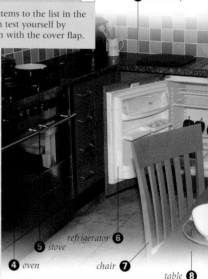

1 *countertop*

1 **die Arbeitsfläche**
dee ar-biets-flay-khe

2 **das Spülbecken**
duss shpewl-bek-ken

3 **die Mikrowelle**
dee mee-kro-vel-le

4 **der Backhofen**
dair bak-oe-fen

5 **der Herd**
dair hairt

6 **der Kühlschrank**
dair kewl-shrunk

7 **der Stuhl**
dair shtool

8 **der Tisch**
dair tish

refrigerator **6**

5 *stove*

4 *oven*   *chair* **7**

table **8**

3 In conversation

Das ist der Herd.
duss isst dair hairt

This is the stove.

**Gibt es eine
Geschirrspül-
maschine?**
geept es ie-ne ge-sheerr-
spewl-mah-shee-ne

Is there a dishwasher?

**Ja, und der
Gefrierschrank ist groß.**
yah, oont dair ge-freer-
shrunk isst groes

*Yes, and the freezer
is big.*

4 Words to remember

Familiarize yourself with these words and test yourself using the flap.

wardrobe	**der Schrank** dair shrunk
armchair	**der Sessel** dair zes-sel
carpet	**der Teppich** dair tep-pikh
bathtub	**die Badewanne** dee bah-de-vunn-ne
toilet	**die Toilette (das WC)** dee twah-let-te (duss vay-tsay)
bathroom sink	**das Waschbecken** duss vush-bek-ken
drapes	**die Gardine** dee gar-dee-ne

Die Couch ist neu.
dee kowtch isst noy
The sofa is new.

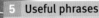
❷ sink

microwave ❸

5 Useful phrases

Learn these phrases and then test yourself.

The stove doesn't work.	**Der Herd funktioniert nicht.** dair hairt foonk-tsee-oe-neert nikht
I don't like the drapes.	**Die Gardinen gefallen mir nicht.** dee gar-dee-nen ge-fall-en meer nikht
Is electricity included?	**Ist der Strom inbegriffen?** isst dair shtroem in-be-grif-fen

6 Say it

Is there a microwave?

I like the carpet.

The bathroom is beautiful!

Ist das Spülbecken neu?
isst duss spewl-bek-ken noy

Is the sink new?

Und hier ist die Waschmaschine.
oont heer isst dee vush-mah-shee-ne

And here's the washing machine.

Die Kacheln sind schön!
dee ka-kheln zint shern

The tiles are beautiful!

1 Warm up

Say "I need" and "you need." (pp.92–3)

What is the German for "day" and "month"? (pp.28–9)

Ask "Is there a garage?" (pp.98–9)

Der Garten
The backyard

Many Germans who live in apartments rent community garden plots. But rather than just growing fruits and vegetables there, they often turn these into attractive gardens with extensive flowerbeds and ponds as well as terraces, decks, and barbecue grills for casual entertaining.

2 Words to remember

Familiarize yourself with these words and test yourself using the flap.

der Rasenmäher dair rah-zen-may-er	*lawnmower*
die Gabel dee gah-bel	*fork*
der Spaten dair shpah-ten	*spade*
der Rechen dair re-khen	*rake*
das Gartencenter duss gar-ten-tsen-ter	*garden center*

❷ *tree*

❸ *soil*

terrace ❶

flowers ❼   *weeds* ❽   ❾ *path*

3 Useful phrases

Learn these phrases and then test yourself using the cover flap.

The gardener comes once a week.	**Der Gärtner kommt einmal in der Woche.** dair gairt-ner komt ine-mahl in dair vo-khe
Can you please mow the lawn?	**Können Sie bitte den Rasen mähen?** kern-nen zee bit-te dayn rah-zen may-en
Is the yard private?	**Ist der Garten privat?** isst dair gar-ten pree-vaht
The garden needs watering.	**Der Garten muss gegossen werden.** dair gar-ten mooss ge-gos-sen vair-den

4 Match and repeat

Match the numbered items in this garden to the words in the panel.

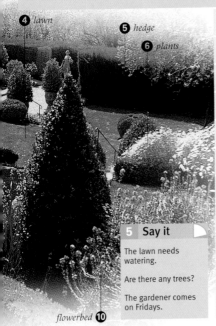

❹ *lawn*
❺ *hedge*
❻ *plants*
flowerbed ❿

1 **die Terrasse** dee ter-ras-se

2 **der Baum** dair bowm

3 **die Erde** dee air-de

4 **der Rasen** dair rah-zen

5 **die Hecke** dee hek-ke

6 **die Pflanzen** dee pflun-tsen

7 **die Blumen** dee bloo-men

8 **das Unkraut** duss oon-krowt

9 **der Weg** dair vayk

10 **das Blumenbeet** duss bloo-men-bayt

5 Say it

The lawn needs watering.

Are there any trees?

The gardener comes on Fridays.

1 Warm up

Say "My name's John". (pp.8–9)

How do you say "don't worry"? (pp.94–5)

What's "your" in German? (pp.12–13)

Die Haustiere
Pets

Many German families have pet animals—dogs and cats are especially popular—and veterinary services are generally of a high standard. Consult your vet for details on the necessary vaccinations and paperwork if you are considering traveling to Germany with your pet.

2 Match and repeat

Match the numbered animals to the German words in the panel on the left. Test yourself using the cover flap.

1 **die Katze**
dee kut-se

2 **das Kaninchen**
duss kah-neen-khen

3 **der Vogel**
dair foe-gel

4 **der Fisch**
dair fish

5 **der Hund**
dair hoont

6 **der Hamster**
dair hums-ter

bird **3**

2 rabbit

1 cat

fish **4**

dog **5**

6 hamster

3 Useful phrases

Familiarize yourself with these phrases and then test yourself using the cover flap.

Ist dieser Hund gutartig? isst dee-zer hoont goot-ar-tikh	*Is this dog friendly?*
Kann ich meinen Hund mitbringen? kunn ikh mie-nen hoont mit-bring-en	*Can I bring my dog?*
Ich habe Angst vor Katzen. ikh hah-be unkst foer kut-tsen	*I'm afraid of cats.*
Mein Hund beißt nicht. mine hoont biesst nikht	*My dog doesn't bite.*

Diese Katze hat Flöhe.
dee-ze kut-se hut fler-we.
This cat has fleas.

Cultural tip Many dogs in Germany are working dogs and you may encounter them tethered or roaming free. Approach rural houses with particular care. Look out for warning notices such as "Warnung vor dem Hunde" (Beware of the dog).

4 Words to remember

Familiarize yourself with these words and test yourself using the flap.

Meinem Hund geht es nicht gut.
mie-nem hoont gayt es nikht goot
My dog is not well.

basket	**der Korb**	dair korp
cage	**der Käfig**	dair kay-fik
bowl	**die Schüssel**	dee shews-sel
collar	**das Halsband**	duss hulls-bunt
leash	**die Leine**	dee lie-ne
vet	**der Tierarzt**	dair teer-artst
vaccination	**die Impfung**	dee imp-foong
pet passport	**der Tierpass**	dair teer-puss
fleas	**die Flöhe**	die fler-we
flea spray	**das Flohspray**	duss flo-shpray

5 Put into practice

Join in this conversation. Read the German on the left and follow the instructions to make your reply. Then test yourself by concealing the answers with the cover flap.

Ist das Ihr Hund?
isst duss eer hoont
Is this your dog?

Say: Yes, he's called Hasso.

Ja, er heißt Hasso.
yah, er hiesst hus-so

Ich habe Angst vor Hunden.
ikh hah-be unkst foer hoon-den
I'm afraid of dogs.

Say: Don't worry, he's well-behaved.

Keine Angst, er ist gutartig.
kie-ne unkst, er isst goot-ar-tikh

Wiederholung
Review and repeat

1 Colors

1 **schwarz**
shvarts

2 **weiß**
vies

3 **rot**
roet

4 **grün**
grewn

5 **gelb**
gelp

1 Colors

Complete the sentences with the German word for the color in brackets.

1 Haben Sie diese Jacke in _____ . (black)

2 Ich nehme den Rock in _____ . (white)

3 Haben Sie die Hose in _____ ? (red)

4 Nein, aber ich habe eine in _____ . (green)

5 Ich möchte diese Schuhe in _____ . (yellow)

2 Kitchen

1 **der Herd**
dair hairt

2 **der Kühlschrank**
dair kewl-shrunk

3 **das Spülbecken**
duss spewl-bek-ken

4 **die Mikrowelle**
dee mee-kro-vel-le

5 **der Backofen**
dair bak-oe-fen

6 **der Stuhl**
dair shtool

7 **der Tisch**
dair tish

2 Kitchen

Say the German words for the numbered items.

❶ *stove*   *refrigerator* ❷

oven ❺   *chair* ❻

3 House

You are being shown around a house in Germany. Join in the conversation, replying in German following the English prompts.

Hier ist das Wohnzimmer.
1 *What a nice sofa.*

Ja, und da ist auch eine große Küche.
2 *How many rooms?*

Es gibt drei Zimmer.
3 *Do you have a garage?*

Nein, aber da ist ein großer Garten.
4 *When is the house available?*

Ab Juli.
5 *What is the rent per month?*

3 House

1 **Was für eine schöne Couch!**
vuss fewr ie-ne shern-ne kowtch

2 **Wie viele Zimmer gibt es?**
vee fee-le tsim-mer geept es

3 **Haben Sie eine Garage?**
hah-ben zee ie-ne ga-ra-je

4 **Ab wann ist das Haus frei?**
up vunn isst duss hows frie

5 **Wie hoch ist die monatliche Miete?**
vee hoekh isst dee mo-naht-li-khe mee-te

4 At home

Say the German for the following items:

1 *washing machine*
2 *sofa*
3 *attic*
4 *dining room*
5 *tree*
6 *garden*

microwave **4**
3 sink
table **7**

4 At home

1 **die Waschmaschine**
dee vush-mah-shee-ne

2 **die Couch**
dee kowtch

3 **der Dachboden**
dair dukh-boe-den

4 **das Esszimmer**
duss es-tsim-mer

5 **der Baum**
dair bowm

6 **der Garten**
dair gar-ten

1 Warm up

Ask "Where can I find the bank?" (pp.68–9)

What's the German for "passport"? (pp.54–5)

Ask "What time?" (pp.30–1)

Bank und Post
Bank and post office

German post offices have machines that print stamps on demand, weigh packages automatically, and explain their services in several languages. Most banks have ATMs with multiple language options. However, banks also offer a teller service, if you need help.

2 Words to remember: post

Familiarize yourself with these words and test yourself using the cover flap to conceal the German on the left.

der Umschlag dair oom-shlahk	*envelope*
die Postkarte dee posst-kar-te	*postcard*
das Paket duss pa-kayt	*package*
per Luftpost pair looft-posst	*by air mail*
per Einschreiben pair ine-shrie-ben	*by registered mail*
der Briefkasten dair breef-kuss-ten	*mailbox*
die Postleitzahl dee posst-lite-tsahl	*postal (ZIP) code*
der Briefträger dair breef-tray-ger	*mail carrier*

Wie hoch ist das Porto nach England?
vee hoekh isst duss por-toe nahkh eng-land
What is the postage to England?

die Briefmarken
dee breef-mar-ken
stamps

3 In conversation

Ich möchte Geld abheben.
ikh merkh-te gelt up-hay-ben

I'd like to withdraw some money.

Können Sie sich ausweisen?
kern-nen zee zikh ows-vie-zen

Do you have any ID?

Ja, ich habe meinen Pass dabei.
Yah, ikh hah-be mye-nen puss da-bie

Yes, I have my passport with me.

4 Words to remember: bank

Familiarize yourself with these words and test yourself using the cover flap to conceal the German on the right.

Wie kann ich zahlen?
vee kunn ikh tsah-len
How can I pay?

PIN	**die Geheimnummer**	dee ge-hime-noom-mer
bank	**die Bank**	dee bunk
teller/cashier	**der Kassierer(in)**	dair kuss-see-rer(in)
ATM	**der Geldautomat**	dair gelt-ow-to-maht
bills (notes)	**die Banknoten**	dee bunk-noe-ten
coin	**die Münze**	dee mewn-tse
credit card	**die Kreditkarte**	dee kray-deet-kar-te

5 Useful phrases

Learn these phrases and then test yourself using the cover flap.

6 Say it

I'd like a stamp.

Where can I find a mailbox?

I have ID.

I'd like to change some money.	**Ich möchte Geld wechseln.** ikh merkh-te gelt wek-seln
What is the exchange rate?	**Wie ist der Wechselkurs?** vee isst dair wek-sel-koors
I'd like to withdraw some money.	**Ich möchte Geld abheben.** ikh merkh-te gelt up-hay-ben

Bitte geben Sie Ihre Geheimzahl ein
bit-te gay-ben zee ee-re ge-hime-tsahl ine

Please type in your PIN.

Muss ich auch unterschreiben?
mooss ikh owkh oon-ter-shrie-ben

Do I need to sign, too?

Nein, das ist nicht nötig.
nine, duss isst nikht ner-tikh

No, that's not necessary.

Dienstleistungen
Services

You can combine the German words on these pages with the vocabulary you learned in week 10 to help you explain basic problems and cope with asking for most repairs. When arranging building work or a repair, it's a good idea to agree on the price and method of payment in advance.

2 Words to remember

Familiarize yourself with these words and test yourself using the flap.

Klempner(in) klemp-ner(in)	*plumber*
Elektriker(in) ay-lek-tree-ker(in)	*electrician*
Mechaniker(in) me-khah-nee-ker(in)	*mechanic*
Bauarbeiter(in) bow-ar-bie-ter(in)	*builder*
die Putzfrau dee poots-frow	*cleaner*
Maler(in) mah-ler(in)	*painter/decorator*
Schreiner(in) shrie-ner(in)	*carpenter*
die Telefonnummer dee tay-lay-foen-noom-mer	*telephone number*

der Radschüssel
dair raht-shlews-sel
tire iron

Ich brauche keinen Mechaniker.
ikh brow-khe kie-nen me-khah-nee-ker.
I don't need a mechanic.

3 In conversation

Die Waschmachine funktioniert nicht.
dee vush-mah-shee-ne foonk-tsee-oen-eert nikht

The washing machine is not working.

Ja, die Pumpe ist kaputt.
yah, dee poom-pe isst ka-poott

Yes, the pipe is broken.

Können Sie die reparieren?
kern-nen zee dee re-pah-ree-ren

Can you repair it?

4 Useful phrases

Learn these phrases and then test yourself using the cover flap.

Can you clean the bathroom?	**Können Sie das Badezimmer putzen?** kern-nen zee duss bah-de-tsim-mer poot-tsen
Can you repair the boiler?	**Können Sie den Boiler reparieren?** kern-nen zee dayn boi-ler re-pah-ree-ren
Do you know a good electrician?	**Kennen Sie einen guten Elektriker?** ken-nen zee ie-nen goo-ten ay-lek-tree-ker

Wo kann ich das reparieren lassen?
voe kunn ikh duss re-pah-ree-ren luss-sen
Where can I get this repaired?

5 Put into practice

Learn these phrases. Cover up the text on the right and complete the dialogue in German. Check your answers and repeat if necessary.

Ihr Tor ist kaputt. eer tohr isst ka-poott *Your gate is broken.*	**Kennen Sie einen guten Handwerker?** ken-nen zee ie-nen goo-ten hunt-ver-ker
Ask: Do you know a good handyman?	
Ja, es gibt einen im Ort. yah, es geept ie-nen im ort *Yes there is one in the village.*	**Haben Sie die Telefonnummer?** hah-ben zee dee tay-lay-foen-noom-mer
Ask: Do you have the telephone number?	

Nein, Sie brauchen eine neue.
nine, zee brow-khen ie-ne noy-e

No, you'll need a new one.

Können Sie das heute machen?
kern-nen zee duss hoy-te ma-khen

Can you do it today?

Nein, ich komme morgen wieder.
nine, ikh kom-me mor-gen vee-der

No. I'll come back tomorrow.

1 Warm up

Say the days of the week in German. (pp.28–9)

How do you say "handyman"? (pp.110–11)

Say "It's 9:30," "10:45," and "12:00." (pp.10–11, pp.30–1)

Kommen
To come

The verb **kommen** (*to come*) is another important verb. Apart from its literal meaning, it can mean "happen" as in "how come?". It can be combined with adverbs such as **her** (*here*) or **herein** (*in*). It also occurs in many expressions, such as **das kommt davon, dass…** (*That's because*).

2 Kommen: to come

Say the different forms of **kommen** (*to come*) aloud. Use the cover flap to test yourself and, when you are confident, practice the sample sentences below.

ich komme ikh kom-me	*I come*
du kommst doo komst	*you come (informal)*
er/sie/es kommt air/zee/es komt	*he/she/it comes*
wir kommen veer kom-men	*we come*
ihr kommt eer komt	*you come (informal, plural)*
sie/Sie kommen zee kom-men	*they come/you come (plural or formal)*
Ich komme aus London. ikh kom-me ows london	*I come from London.*
Wir kommen jeden Dienstag. veer kom-men yay-den deens-tahk	*We come every Tuesday.*
Sie kommen mit dem Zug. zee kom-men mit daym tsook	*They come by train*

Er kommt aus China.
air komt ows khee-nah
He comes from China.

Conversational tip "Kommen" is used in many (usually friendly) commands such as "komm her" (come here) or "kommen Sie herein" (come in). It also often appears together with another verb, when in English we might link the two verbs with "and," as in: "komm setz dich" (come and sit down), "kommt essen" (come and eat).

3 Useful phrases

Learn these phrases and then test yourself using the cover flap.

When can I come?	**Wann kann ich kommen?** vunn kunn ikh kom-men
Where does she come from?	**Woher kommt sie?** vo-hair komt zee
The cleaner comes every Monday.	**Die Putzfrau kommt jeden Montag.** dee poots-frow komt yay-den moen-tahk
Come with me. (informal/formal)	**Komm mit/ Kommen Sie mit.** kom mit/ kom-men zee mit

Bitte setzen Sie sich.
bit-te zet-sen zee zikh
Come and sit down.

4 Put into practice

Join in this conversation. Read the German on the left and follow the instructions to make your reply. Then test yourself by concealing the answers with the cover flap.

Guten Tag, Friseur-salon Hannelore.
goo-ten tahk, fri-zer-zah-long hun-ne-loe-re
Hello, this is Hannelore's hair salon.

Say: I'd like an appointment.

Ich hätte gern einen Termin.
ikh het-te gairn ie-nen terr-meen

Wann möchten Sie kommen?
vunn merkh-ten zee kom-men

Say: Can I come today?

Kann ich heute kommen?
kunn ikh hoy-te kom-men

Natürlich. Um wieviel Uhr?
na-tewr-likh. oomm vee-feel oor
Yes, of course. What time?

Say: At 10.30.

Um halb elf.
oomm hulp elf

Polizei und Verbrechen
Police and crime

German traffic police (**Verkehrspolizei**) carry out checks and impose fines for violations of the traffic regulations. If you are the victim of a crime or are in a traffic accident in Germany, report it to the nearest police station.

2 Words to remember: crime

Familiarize yourself with these words.

der Diebstahl dair deep-shtahl	*robbery*
der Polizeibericht dair po-lee-tsie-be-rikht	*police report*
der Dieb dair deep	*thief*
die Polizei dee po-lee-tsie	*police*
die Aussage dee ows-zah-ge	*statement*
Rechtsanwalt/-wältin rekhts-un-vullt/-vael-tin	*lawyer*
Zeuge/Zeugin tsoy-ge/tsoy-gin	*witness*

Ich brauche einen Rechtsanwalt.
ikh brow-khe ie-nen rekhts-un-vullt
I need a lawyer.

3 Useful phrases

Memorize these phrases and then test yourself.

Ich bin bestohlen worden. ikh bin be-shtoe-len vor-den	*I've been robbed.*
Was ist gestohlen worden? vuss isst ge-shtoe-len vor-den	*What was stolen?*
Haben Sie den Täter gesehen? hah-ben zee den tay-ter ge-zay-en	*Did you see who did it?*
Wann ist es passiert? vunn isst es puss-seert	*When did it happen?*

die Wertsachen
dee vairt-zakh-en
valuables

4 Words to remember: appearance

Learn these words for describing people.

Er hat eine Glatze und einen Bart.
air hut ie-ne glut-se oont ie-nen bart
He is bald and has and a beard.

Er hat kurze, schwarze Haare.
air hut koor-tse, shvar-tse hah-re
He has short, black hair.

man	**der Mann**	dair munn
woman	**die Frau**	dee frow
tall	**groß**	groes
short	**klein**	kline
young	**jung**	yoong
old	**alt**	ullt
fat	**dick**	dick
thin	**dünn**	dewnn
long/short hair	**lange/kurze Haare**	lun-ge/koor-tse hah-re
glasses	**die Brille**	dee bril-le
beard	**der Bart**	dair bart

■■ Cultural tip If you have a car accident or serious breakdown on an expressway, use one of the special telephones that you can find at regular intervals. Elsewhere, call 112, which is free from all telephones in Germany. The operator will inform the appropriate service (police, fire service, or ambulance) immediately.

---

5 Put into practice

Practice these phrases. Then cover up the text on the right and follow the instructions to make your reply in German.

Wie sah er aus?
vee zah air ows
What did he look like?

Say: Short and fat.

Klein und dick.
kline oont dick

Und die Haare?
oont dee hah-re
And the hair?

Say: Long, with a beard.

Lang, mit Bart.
lung, mit bart

Wiederholung
Review and repeat

1 To come

1 komme
   kom-me

2 kommt
   komt

3 kommen
   kom-men

4 kommt
   komt

5 kommen
   kom-men

1 To come

Fill in the gaps with the correct form of
kommen (*to come*).

1 Ich _____ um vier Uhr.

2 Der Gärtner _____ einmal in der Woche.

3 Wir _____ Dienstag zum Essen.

4 _____ ihr mit?

5 Meine Eltern _____ mit dem Zug.

2 Bank and mail

1 die Banknoten
   dee bunk-noe-ten

2 die Postkarte
   dee posst-kar-te

3 das Paket
   duss pa-kayt

4 die Briefmarken
   dee breef-mar-ken

2 Bank and mail

Name the numbered items in German.

❶ bills (notes)

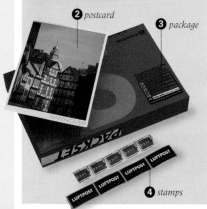

❷ postcard

❸ package

❹ stamps

3 Appearance

What do these descriptions mean?

1 **Der Mann ist groß und dünn.**

2 **Sie hat kurze Haare und eine Brille.**

3 **Ich bin klein und habe lange Haare.**

4 **Sie ist alt und dick.**

5 **Er hat blaue Augen und einen Bart.**

3 Appearance

1 *The man is tall and thin.*

2 *She has short hair and glasses.*

3 *I'm short and I have long hair.*

4 *She is old and fat.*

5 *He has blue eyes and a beard.*

4 The pharmacy

You are asking a pharmacist for advice. Join in the conversation, replying in German where you see the English prompts.

Guten Tag, kann ich Ihnen helfen?
1 *I have a cough.*

Und haben Sie auch Schnupfen?
2 *No, but I have a headache.*

Nehmen Sie diese Tabletten.
3 *Do you have that as a syrup?*

Selbstverständlich. Bitte sehr.
4 *Thank you. How much is that?*

Sechs Euro.
5 *Here you are. Goodbye.*

4 The pharmacy

1 **Ich habe Husten.**
ikh hah-be hoos-ten

2 **Nein, aber ich habe Kopfschmerzen.**
nine, ah-ber ikh hah-be kopf-shmairt-sen

3 **Haben Sie das auch als Sirup?**
hah-ben zee duss owkh ulls zee-roop

4 **Danke. Was macht das?**
dun-ke. vuss mukht duss

5 **Bitte sehr. Auf Wiedersehen.**
bit-te zair. owf vee-der-zay-en

Die Freizeit
Leisure time

In Germany the arts, from opera and classic drama to performance art and cabaret, and from great composers to folk and avant-garde music, are avidly followed and receive public support. **Lust haben** is a useful expression, meaning to like the idea of doing something.

2 Words to remember

Familiarize yourself with these words.

das Theater duss tay-ah-ter	*theater*
das Kino duss kee-no	*movie theater*
das Ballett duss bull-let	*ballet*
die Musik dee moo-zeek	*music*
die Kunst dee koonst	*art*
der Sport dair shport	*sports*
die Besichtigungen dee be-zikh-tee-goong-en	*sightseeing*
die Computerspiele dee com-pyoo-ter-shpee-le	*computer games*

Ich liebe Opern.
ikh lee-be oh-pairn
I love opera.

das Publikum
duss poo-blee-koomm
audience

3 In conversation

Hast du Lust, heute Tennis zu spielen?
husst doo loost, hoy-te ten-nis tsoo shpee-len

Do you want to play tennis today?

Nein, ich mag keinen Sport.
nine, ikh mahk kie-nen shport

No, I don't like sports.

Wofür interessierst du dich denn?
voe-fewr in-ter-es-seerst doo dikh den

So what are you interested in?

4 Useful phrases

Learn these phrases and then test yourself using the cover flap.

Ich hasse Gitarrenmusik.
ikh hus-se gee-tar-ren-moo-zeek
I hate guitar music.

der Rang
dair rung
balcony

das Parkett
duss par-ket
orchestra level

I like the theater.	**Ich liebe das Theater.** ikh lee-be duss tay-ah-ter
I prefer the movies.	**Ich ziehe das Kino vor.** ikh tsee-e duss kee-no for
I'm interested in art.	**Ich interessiere mich für die Kunst.** ikh in-ter-es-see-re mikh fewr dee koonst
What are your (formal/informal) interests?	**Wofür interessierst du dich/interessieren Sie sich?** vo-fewr in-ter-es-seerst doo dikh/in-ter-es-see-ren zee zikh
That bores me.	**Das finde ich langweilig.** duss fin-de ikh lung-vie-likh

5 Say it

I'm interested in music.

I prefer sports.

I don't like computer games.

Ich mache lieber Besichtigungen.
ikh ma-khe lee-ber be-zikh-tee-goong-en

I prefer sightseeing.

Das interessiert mich nicht.
duss in-ter-es-seert mikh nikht

That doesn't interest me.

Kein Problem. Ich gehe allein.
kine pro-blaym. ikh gay-he ull-line

No problem. I'll go on my own.

1 Warm up

Ask "Do you (informal) want to play tennis?" (pp.118–19)

Say "I like the movies," "I prefer sightseeing," and "That doesn't interest me." (pp.118–19)

Sport und Hobbys
Sports and hobbies

Germany is a nation of sports enthusiasts. Many people cycle, jog, swim, or work out at the gym, and many follow sports as spectators. Soccer is very popular, but so are boxing, hockey, tennis, and skiing. The verb **Spielen** (*to play*) is mainly used for ball games.

2 Words to remember: sports

Familiarize yourself with these words and test yourself using the flap.

der Fußball dair foos-bull	*soccer*
das Boxen duss box-en	*boxing*
das Tennis duss ten-nis	*tennis*
das Schwimmen duss shvim-men	*swimming*
das Segeln duss zay-geln	*sailing*
das Angeln duss ung-eln	*fishing*
das Radfahren duss raht-fah-ren	*cycling*
das Wandern duss vunn-dairn	*hiking*

der Bunker
dair boon-ker
bunker

der Golfspieler
dair golf-shpee-ler
golfer

Ich spiele jeden Tag Golf.
ikh shpee-le yay-den tahk golf
I play golf every day.

3 Useful phrases

Familiarize yourself with these phrases.

Ich spiele Fußball. ikh shpee-le foos-bull	*I play soccer.*
Wir spielen gern Tennis. veer shpee-len gairn ten-nis.	*We like playing tennis.*
Sie malt. zee mahlt.	*She paints.*

4 Words to remember: hobbies

Learn these words and phrases, then test yourself using the cover flap.

Ich begesitere mich für das Fotografieren.
ikh be-gesi-tair mikh fewr foe-to-grah-fee-ayren
I'm into photography.

die Flagge
dee flug-ge
flag

der Golfplatz
dair golf-pluts
golf course

das Basteln duss bass-teln	*do-it-yourself*
die Töpferei dee ter-pfe-rie	*pottery*
das Blumenstecken duss bloo-men-shtek-en	*flower arranging*
die Gartenarbeit dee gar-ten-ar-biet	*gardening*
das Singen duss zing-en	*singing*
Kann ich einem Klub beitreten? kunn ikh ien-em kloop bie-tray-ten	*Can I join a club?*
Muss man Mitglied sein? moos munn mit-gleet zine	*Do I have to be a member?*
Kann ich die Ausrüstung mieten? kumm ikh dee ows-rews-toong mee-ten	*Can I rent the equipment?*

5 Put into practice

Join in this conversation. Conceal the text on the right and complete the dialogue in German using the cover flap. Check your answers.

Was machst du gern?
vuss mukhst doo gairn
What do you like doing?

Say: *I like playing tennis.*

Ich spiele gern Tennis.
ikh shpee-le gairn ten-nis

Spielst du auch Golf?
speelst doo owkh golf
Do you also play golf?

Say: *No, I play soccer.*

Nein, ich spiele Fußball.
nine, ikh shpee-le foos-bull

Spielst du oft?
speelst doo oft
Do you play often?

Say: *Yes, I play every week.*

Ja, ich spiele jede Woche.
yah, ikh shpee-le yay-de vokh-e

Besuchen
Socializing

1 Warm up

Say "my husband" and "my wife." (pp.10–11)

How do you say "lunch" and "dinner" in German? (pp.20–1)

Say "Sorry, I'm busy." (pp.32–3)

In Germany, much socializing takes place outside the home. People meet to go to a play, a movie, or a sports event together, or they go out for a meal or a drink. Friends and family also invite each other for meals, especially for special occasions such as birthdays.

2 Useful phrases

Learn these phrases and then test yourself.

Ich möchte Sie zum Abendessen einladen. ikh merkh-te zee tsoom ah-bent-ess-sen ine-lah-den	*I'd like to invite you for dinner.*
Sind Sie nächsten Mittwoch frei? zint zee nayks-ten mit-vokh frie	*Are you free next Wednesday?*
Vielleicht ein andermal. feel-liekht ine un-der-mahl	*Perhaps another time.*

Cultural tip When you go to someone's house for the first time, flowers are a welcome gift. If you are invited again, being better acquainted, you can bring something a little more personal.

3 In conversation

Möchten Sie zum Mittagessen kommen? merkh-ten zee tsoom mit-tahk-ess-sen kom-men

Would you like to come to lunch?

Mit Vergnügen. Wann? mit fer-g-new-gen. vunn

I'd be delighted. When?

Wie wär's mit Donnerstag? vee vairs mit don-ners-tahk

How about Thursday?

4 Words to remember

Familiarize yourself with these words and test yourself using the flap.

die Gastgeberin
dee gust-gay-be-rin
hostess

der Gast
dair gust
guest

party	**die Party** dee par-tee
dinner party	**das Abendessen** duss ah-bent-ess-sen
invitation	**die Einladung** dee ine-lah-doong
reception	**der Empfang** dair emp-fung
cocktail party	**die Cocktailparty** dee kock-tayl-par-tee

5 Put into practice

Join in this conversation.

Danke für die Einladung.
dun-ke fewr dee ine-lah-doonk.
Thank you for inviting us.

Können Sie heute Abend zu einem Empfang kommen? ker-nen zee hoy-te ah-bent tsoo ie-nem emp-fung kom-men *Can you come to a reception tonight?*	**Ja, gerne.** yah, gair-ne
Say: Yes, I'd love to.	
Es fängt um zwanzig Uhr an. es fengt oom tsvun-tsik oor un *It starts at eight o'clock.*	**Was trägt man?** vuss traygt munn
Ask: What should I wear?	

Das passt mir gut.
duss pusst meer goot

That's good for me.

Bringen Sie Ihren Mann mit.
brin-gen zee ee-ren munn mit

Bring your husband.

Danke. Um wieviel Uhr?
dun-ke. oom vee-feel oor

Thank you. What time?

Wiederholung
Review and repeat

Antworten
Answers
Cover with flap

1 Animals

1 **der Fisch**
dair fish

2 **der Vogel**
dair foh-gel

3 **das Kaninchen**
duss kah-neen-khen

4 **die Katze**
dee kut-se

5 **der Hamster**
dair hums-ter

6 **der Hund**
dair hoont

1 Animals

Name the animals.

1 *fish*

bird **2**

hamster **5**

4 *cat*

2 I like...

1 **Ich spiele gern Fußball.**
ikh shpee-le gairn foos-bull

2 **Ich spiele nicht gern Golf.**
ikh shpee-le nikht gairn golf

3 **Ich male gern.**
ikh mah-le gairn

4 **Blumenstecken mache ich nicht gern.**
bloo-men-shtek-ken makh-e ikh nikht gairn

2 I like...

Say the following in German.

1 *I like playing soccer.*

2 *I don't like playing golf.*

3 *I like to paint.*

4 *I don't like flower arranging.*

3 *rabbit*

6 *dog*

3 Leisure

What is the German for these sports and leisure activities?

1 *sailing*

2 *art*

3 *sightseeing*

4 *movies*

5 *hiking*

6 *swimming*

3 Leisure

1 **das Segeln**
duss zay-geln

2 **die Kunst**
dee koonst

3 **die Besichtigungen**
dee be-zikh-tee-goong-en

4 **das Kino**
duss kee-no

5 **das Wandern**
duss vunn-dairn

6 **das Schwimmen**
duss shvim-men

4 An invitation

You are invited for dinner. Join in the conversation, replying in German following the English prompts.

Möchten Sie am Freitag zum Essen kommen?
1 *I'm sorry, I'm busy.*

Wie wär's mit Samstag?
2 *I'd love to.*

Bringen Sie Ihre Kinder mit.
3 *Thank you. What time?*

Um halb eins.
4 *That's good for me.*

4 An invitation

1 **Es tut mir Leid, ich habe schon etwas vor.**
es toot meer liet, ikh hah-be shoen et-vuss for

2 **Mit Vergnügen.**
mit fer-g-new-gen

3 **Danke. Um wieviel Uhr?**
dun-ke. oom vee-feel oor

4 **Ja, das passt mir.**
yah, duss pusst meer

Reinforce and progress

Regular practice is the key to maintaining and advancing
your language skills. In this section you will find a variety
of suggestions for reinforcing and extending your knowledge
of German. Many involve returning to exercises in the
book and using the dictionaries to extend their scope.
Go back through the lessons in a different order, mix and
match activities to make up your own 15-minute daily
program, or focus on topics that are of particular relevance
to your current needs.

Keep warmed up
Revisit the Warm Up boxes to remind yourself of
key words and phrases. Make sure you work your
way through all of them on a regular basis.

1 Warm up

Say "I'm sorry."
(pp.32–3)

What is the German
for "I'd like an
appointment"?
(pp.32–3)

Ask "with whom?" in
German. (pp.32–3)

2 I'd like...

Say you'd like the following:

cake ❶

coffee ❸

❷ *black tea*

Review and repeat again
Work through a Review and Repeat
lesson as a way of reinforcing
words and phrases presented in
the course. Return to the main
lesson for any topic on which you
are no longer confident.

3 In conversation: taxi

Carry on conversing
Reread the In
Conversation panels.
Say both parts of the
conversation, paying
attention to the
pronunciation.
Where possible, try
incorporating new
words from the
dictionary.

Zum Flughafen, bitte.
tsoom flook-hah-fen,
bit-te

The airport, please.

Jawohl, kein Problem.
yah-voel, kine pro-blaym

Yes, no problem.

Können Sie mich
hier absetsen?
ker-nen zee mikh bi
heer up-zet-sen

Can you drop me
please?

4 Useful phrases

Learn these phrases and then test yourself using the cover flap.

Öffnungszeiten: Di. - Fr. 11 - 18 Uhr Sa. + So. 11 - 16 Uhr (Montags geschlossen)	*What time do you* *open/close?*	**Wann öffnen/** **schließen Sie?** vunn erf-nen/shlee-sen zee
Toilette	*Where are the* *restrooms?*	**Wo sind die** **Toiletten?** voe zind dee twah-let-ten
	Is there wheelchair *access?*	**Gibt es Zugang für** **Rollstuhlfahrer?** geept es tsoo-gung fewr roll-shtool-fah-rer

Practice phrases
Return to the Useful
Phrases and Put into
Practice exercises.
Test yourself using
the cover flap. When
you are confident,
devise your own
versions of the
phrases, using new
words from the
dictionary.

Match, repeat, and extend
Remind yourself of words related to specific topics by returning to the Match and Repeat and Words to Remember exercises. Test yourself using the cover flap. Discover new words in that area by referring to the dictionary and menu guide.

5 Match and repeat

Match the numbered items in this scene with the text in the panel.

1 **der Rhabarber**
dair ra-bar-ber

2 **die Kartoffeln**
dee kar-toff-eln

3 **die Radieschen**
dee ra-dees-khen

4 **der Spinat**
dair shpee-naht

5 **die Möhren**
dee mer-ren

6 **der Kohl**
dair koel

7 **die Lauche**
dee low-khe

8 **der Kohlrabi**
dair koel-rah-bee

potatoes ❷   ❸ radishes
rhubarb ❶   ❹ spinach

❺ carrots

cabbage ❻   ❽ kohlrabi
❼ leeks

6 Say it

The lawn needs watering.

Are there any trees?

The gardener comes on Fridays.

Say it again
The Say It exercises are a useful instant reminder for each lesson. Practice these, using your own vocabulary variations from the dictionary or elsewhere in the lesson.

Using other resources

In addition to working with this book, try the following language extension ideas:

• Visit a German-speaking country and try out your new skills with native speakers. Find out if there is a German community near you. There may be shops, cafés, restaurants, and clubs. Try to visit some of these and use your German to order food and drink and strike up conversations. Most native speakers will be happy to speak German to you.

• Join a language class or club. There are usually evening and day classes available at a variety of different levels. Or you could start a club yourself if you have friends who are also interested in keeping up their German.

• Look at German magazines and newspapers. The pictures will help you to understand the text. Advertisements are also a useful way of expanding your vocabulary.

• Use the Internet, where you can find all kinds of websites for learning languages, some of which offer free online help and activities. You can also find German websites for anything from renting a house to shampooing your pet. You can even access German radio and TV stations online. Start by going to a German search engine, such as *excite.de*, and keying a subject that interests you, or set yourself a challenge: for example, finding a two-bedroom apartment for rent in Hamburg.

Menu guide

This guide lists the most common terms you may encounter on German menus or when shopping for food. If you can't find an exact phrase, try looking up its component parts.

A

Aal *eel*
am Spieß *on the spit*
Ananas *pineapple*
Äpfel *apple*
Apfel im Schlafrock *baked apple in puff pastry*
Apfelsaft *apple juice*
Apfelsinen *oranges*
Apfelstrudel *apple strudel*
Apfeltasche *apple turnover*
Apfelwein *cider*
Aprikosen *apricots*
Arme Ritter *bread soaked in milk and egg then fried*
Artischocken *artichokes*
Auberginen *eggplant*
Auflauf *baked pudding or omelet*
Aufschnitt *cold meats*
Austern *oysters*

B

Backobst *dried fruit*
Backpflaume *prune*
Baiser *meringue*
Balkansalat *cabbage and pepper salad*
Bananen *bananas*
Bandnudeln *ribbon noodles*
Basilikum *basil*
Bauernauflauf *bacon and potato omelet*
Bauernfrühstück *fried potato, bacon, and egg*
Bauernomelett *bacon and potato omelet*
Bechamelkartoffeln *potatoes in creamy sauce*
Bedienung *service*
Beilagen *side dishes*
Berliner *jelly doughnut*
Bier *beer*
Birnen *pears*
Biskuit *sponge cake*
Bismarckhering *filleted pickled herring*
Blätterteig *puff pastry*
blau *cooked in vinegar; virtually raw (steak)*
Blumenkohl *cauliflower*
blutig *rare*
Blutwurst *black pudding*
Bockwurst *large frankfurter*
Bohnen *beans*

Bouillon *clear soup*
Braten *roast meat*
Brathering *pickled and fried herring, served cold*
Bratkartoffeln *fried potatoes*
Bratwurst *grilled pork sausage*
Brot *bread*
Brötchen *roll*
Brühwurst *large frankfurter*
Brust *breast*
Bückling *smoked red herring*
Buletten *burgers; rissoles*
Bunte Platte *mixed platter*
Burgundersoße *Burgundy wine sauce*
Buttercremetorte *cream cake*
Buttermilch *buttermilk*

C, D

Champignons *mushrooms*
Cordon bleu *veal cordon bleu*
Currywurst mit Pommes frites *curried pork sausage with fries*
Dampfnudeln *sweet yeast dumpling*
Deutsches Beefsteak *ground meat or patty*
Dicke Bohnen *broad beans*
Dillsoße *dill sauce*
durchgebraten *well-done*
durchwachsen *with fat*
durchwachsener Speck *bacon*

E

Eier *eggs*
Eierauflauf *omelet*
Eierkuchen *pancake*
Eierpfannkuchen *pancake*
Eierspeise *egg dish*
eingelegt *pickled*
Eintopf *stew*
Eintopfgericht *stew*
Eis *ice*
Eisbecher *sundae*
Eisbein *knuckles of pork*
Eisschokolade *iced chocolate*
Eissplittertorte *ice chip cake*

Endiviensalat *endive salad*
englisch *rare*
Entenbraten *roast duck*
entgrätet *bones (fish)*
Erbsen *peas*
Erdbeertorte *strawberry cake*
Essig *vinegar*

F

Falscher Hase *meat loaf*
Fasan *pheasant*
Fenchel *fennel*
Fett *fat*
Filet *fillet (steak)*
Fisch *fish*
Fischfrikadellen *fishcakes*
Fischstäbchen *fish sticks*
Flädlesuppe *consommé with crepe strips*
flambiert *flambéed*
Fleischbrühe *bouillon*
Fleischkäse *meat loaf*
Fleischklößchen *meatball(s)*
Fleischpastete *meat vol-au-vent*
Fleischsalat *diced meat salad with mayonnaise*
Fleischwurst *pork sausage*
Fond *meat juices*
Forelle *trout*
Forelle Müllerin (Art) *breaded trout with butter and lemon*
Frikadelle *rissole*
Frikassee *fricassee*
fritiert *(deep-) fried*
Froschschenkel *frog's legs*
Fruchtsaft *fruit juice*
Frühlingsrolle *spring roll*

G

Gans *goose*
Gänseleberpastete *goose-liver pâté*
garniert *garnished*
Gebäck *pastries, cakes*
gebacken *baked*
gebraten *roast*
gedünstet *steamed*
Geflügel *poultry*
Geflügelleberragout *chicken liver ragoût*
gefüllt *stuffed*

gefüllte Kalbsbrust *veal roll*
gekocht *boiled*
Gelee *gelatin*
gemischter Salat *mixed salad*
Gemüse *vegetable(s)*
Gemüseplatte *assorted vegetables*
gepökelt *salted, pickled*
geräuchert *smoked*
Gericht *dish*
geschmort *braised, stewed*
Geschnetzeltes *strips of fried meat in cream sauce*
gespickt *larded*
Getränke *beverages*
Gewürze *spices*
Gewürzgurken *pickles*
Goldbarsch *type of perch*
Götterspeise *jelly*
gratiniert *au gratin*
Grieß *semolina*
Grießklößchen *semolina dumplings*
grüne Bohnen *French beans*
grüne Nudeln *green pasta*
grüner Aal *fresh eel*
Grünkohl *(curly) kale*
Gulasch *goulash*
Gulaschsuppe *goulash soup*
Gurkensalat *cucumber salad*

H

Hackfleisch *ground meat*
Hähnchen *chicken*
Hähnchenkeule *chicken leg*
Haifischflossensuppe *shark-fin soup*
Hammelbraten *roast mutton*
Hammelfleisch *mutton*
Hammelkeule *leg of mutton*
Hammelrücken *saddle of mutton*
Hartkäse *hard cheese*
Haschee *hash*
Hasenkeule *haunch of hare*
Hasenpfeffer *hare casserole*
Hauptspeisen *main courses*
Hecht *pike*
Heidelbeeren *bilberries, blueberries*
Heilbutt *halibut*
Heringsstipp *herring salad*
Heringstopf *pickled herrings in sauce*
Herz *heart*
Herzragout *heart ragoût*
Himbeeren *raspberries*
Himmel und Erde *potato*

and apple purée with black pudding or liver sausage
Hirn *brains*
Hirschbraten *roast venison*
Honig *honey*
Honigmelone *honeydew melon*
Hoppelpoppel *bacon and potato omelet*
Hüfte *haunch*
Huhn *chicken*
Hühnerbrühe *chicken broth*
Hühnerfrikassee *chicken fricassee*
Hülsenfrüchte *peas and beans, legumes*
Hummer *lobster*

J, K

Jägerschnitzel *cutlet with mushrooms*
Kabeljau *cod*
Kaffee *coffee*
Kaiserschmarren *sugared pancake with raisins*
Kakao *cocoa*
Kalbfleisch *veal*
Kalbsbries *sweetbread*
Kalbsfrikassee *veal fricassee*
Kalbshaxe *leg of veal*
Kalbsnierenbraten *roast veal with kidney*
Kalbsschnitzel *veal cutlet*
kalte Platte *cold platter*
kaltes Büfett *cold buffet*
Kaltschale *cold, sweet fruit soup*
Kaninchen *rabbit*
Kapern *capers*
Karamelpudding *caramel pudding*
Karotten *carrots*
Karpfen *carp*
Kartoffelbrei *mashed potato*
Kartoffeln *potatoes*
Kartoffelpuffer *potato fritters*
Kartoffelpüree *mashed potato*
Käse *cheese*
Käsegebäck *cheese crackers*
Käsekuchen *cheesecake*
Käseplatte *selection of cheeses*
Käse-Sahne-Torte *cream cheesecake*
Käsespätzle *homemade noodles with cheese*
Kasseler Rippenspeer *smoked pork loin*
Kasserolle *casserole*
Kassler *smoked pork loin*
Kastanien *chestnuts*
Katenrauchwurst *smoked sausage*

Keule *leg, haunch*
Kieler Sprotten *smoked sprats*
Kirschen *cherries*
klare Brühe *consommé*
Klöße *dumplings*
Knäckebrot *crispbread*
Knacker *spicy fried sausage*
Knackwurst *spicy fried sausage*
Knoblauch *garlic*
Knochen *bone*
Knochenschinken *ham on the bone*
Knödel *dumplings*
Kognak *brandy*
Kohl *cabbage*
Kohlrouladen *stuffed cabbage leaves*
Kohl und Pinkel *cabbage, potatoes, sausage, and smoked meat*
Kompott *stewed fruit*
Konfitüre *jam*
Königinpastete *chicken vol-au-vent*
Königsberger Klopse *meatballs in caper sauce*
Königskuchen *type of fruit cake*
Kopfsalat *lettuce*
Kotelett *chop*
Krabben *shrimp*
Krabbencocktail *shrimp cocktail*
Kraftbrühe *beef consommé*
Kräuter *herbs*
Krautsalat *coleslaw*
Krautwickel *stuffed cabbage leaves*
Krebs *crayfish*
Kresse *cress*
Kroketten *croquettes*
Kruste *crust*
Kuchen *cake*
Kürbis *pumpkin*

L

Labskaus *meat, fish, and potato stew*
Lachs *salmon*
Lachsersatz *sliced, salted pollack (fish)*
Lachsforelle *sea trout*
Lachsschinken *smoked rolled fillet of ham*
Lamm *lamb*
Lammrücken *saddle of lamb*
Langusten *crayfish*
Lauch *leek*
Leber *liver*
Leberkäse *baked pork and beef loaf*
Leberpastete *liver pâté*
Leberwurst *liver pâté*
Lebkuchen *gingerbread*
Leipziger Allerlei *mixed vegetables*
Linsen *lentils*

M

mager *lean*
Majoran *marjoram*
Makrele *mackerel*
Makronen *macaroons*
Mandeln *almonds*
mariniert *marinaded, pickled*
Markklößchen *marrow dumplings*
Marmelade *jam*
Maronen *sweet chestnuts*
Matjes(hering) *young herring*
Medaillons *small fillets*
Meeresfische *seafish*
Meeresfrüchte *seafood*
Meerrettich *horseradish*
Miesmuscheln *mussels*
Milch *milk*
Milchmixgetränk *milk shake*
Milchreis *rice pudding*
Mineralwasser *(sparkling) mineral water*
Mohnkuchen *poppyseed cake*
Möhren *carrots*
Mohrrüben *carrots*
Most *fruit wine*
Mus *purée*
Muscheln *mussels*
Muskat(nuss) *nutmeg*
MWSt (Mehrwertsteuer) *VAT*

N, O

nach Art des Hauses *of the house*
nach Hausfrauenart *homemade*
Nachspeisen *desserts*
Nachtisch *dessert*
Napfkuchen *ring-shaped poundcake*
natürlich *natural*
Nieren *kidneys*
Nudeln *pasta, noodles*
Nüsse *nuts*
Obstsalat *fruit salad*
Ochsenschwanzsuppe *oxtail soup*
Öl *oil*
Oliven *olives*
Orangen *oranges*
Orangensaft *orange juice*

P

Palatschinken *stuffed pancakes*
paniert *with breadcrumbs*
Paprika *peppers*
Paprikaschoten *peppers*
Paradiesäpfel *tomatoes*
Pastete *vol-au-vent*
Pellkartoffeln *potatoes boiled in their skins*

Petersilie *parsley*
Pfannkuchen *pancake(s)*
Pfeffer *pepper*
Pfifferlinge *chanterelles*
Pfirsiche *peaches*
Pflaumen *plums*
Pflaumenkuchen *plum tart*
Pflaumenmus *plum jam*
Pichelsteiner Topf *vegetable stew with beef*
pikant *spicy*
Pilze *mushrooms*
Platte *selection*
pochiert *poached*
Pökelfleisch *salt meat*
Pommes frites *French fried potatoes*
Porree *leek*
Potthast *braised beef with sauce*
Poularde *young chicken*
Preiselbeeren *cranberries*
Presskopf *brawn*
Pumpernickel *black rye bread*
Püree *mashed potato*
püriert *puréed*
Putenschenkel *turkey leg*
Puter *turkey*

Q, R

Quark *curd cheese*
Radieschen *radishes*
Rahm *(sour) cream*
Räucheraal *smoked eel*
Räucherhering *kipper, smoked herring*
Räucherlachs *smoked salmon*
Räucherspeck *smoked bacon*
Rauchfleisch *smoked meat*
Rehbraten *roast venison*
Rehgulasch *venison goulash*
Rehkeule *haunch of venison*
Rehrücken *saddle of venison*
Reibekuchen *potato waffles*
Reis *rice*
Reisbrei *creamed rice*
Reisrand *with rice*
Remoulade *mayonnaise flavored with herbs, mustard, and capers*
Renke *whitefish*
Rettich *radish*
Rhabarber *rhubarb*
Rheinischer Sauerbraten *roast pickled beef*
Rinderbraten *pot roast*
Rinderfilet *fillet steak*
Rinderrouladen *beef olives*

Rinderzunge *ox tongue*
Rindfleisch *beef*
Rippchen *spareribs*
Risi-Pisi *rice and peas*
roh *raw*
Rohkostplatte *selection of salads*
Rollmops *rolled-up pickled herring, rollmops*
rosa *rare to medium*
Rosenkohl *Brussels sprouts*
Rosinen *raisins*
Rostbraten *roast*
Rostbratwurst *barbecued sausage*
Rösti *fried potatoes and onions*
Röstkartoffeln *fried potatoes*
Rotbarsch *type of perch*
Rote Bete *beet*
rote Grütze *red fruit jelly*
Rotkohl *red cabbage*
Rotkraut *red cabbage*
Rotwein *red wine*
Rühreier *scrambled eggs*
Russische Eier *hard-boiled egg and mayonnaise*

S

Sahne *cream*
Salate *salads*
Salatplatte *selection of salads*
Salatsoße *salad dressing*
Salz *salt*
Salzburger Nockerln *sweet soufflés*
Salzheringe *salted herrings*
Salzkartoffeln *boiled potatoes*
Salzkruste *salty crusted skin*
Sandkuchen *type of Madeira cake*
sauer *sour*
Sauerbraten *roast pickled beef*
Sauerkraut *pickled white cabbage*
Sauerrahm *sour cream*
Schaschlik *(shish-)kebab*
Schattenmorellen *morello cherries*
Schellfisch *haddock*
Schildkrötensuppe *real turtle soup*
Schillerlocken *smoked haddock rolls*
Schinken *ham*
Schinkenröllchen *rolled ham*
Schlachtplatte *selection of fresh sausages*
Schlagsahne *whipped cream*
Schlei *tench*

Schmorbraten *pot roast*
Schnecken *snails*
Schnittlauch *chives*
Schnitzel *breaded escalope*
Schokolade *chocolate*
Scholle *plaice*
Schulterstück *slice of shoulder*
Schwarzbrot *brown rye bread*
Schwarzwälder Kirschtorte *Black Forest cake*
Schwarzwurzeln *salsify*
Schwein *pork*
Schweinebauch *belly of pork*
Schweinefleisch *pork*
Schweinerippe *cured pork chop*
Schweinerollbraten *rolled roast of pork*
Schweineschmorbraten *roast pork*
Schweineschnitzel *breaded pork cutlet*
Schweinshaxe *knuckle of pork*
Seelachs *pollack (fish)*
Seezunge *sole*
Sekt *sparkling wine*
Sellerie *celeriac*
Semmel *bread roll*
Senf *mustard*
Senfsahnesoße *mustard and cream sauce*
Senfsoße *mustard sauce*
Serbisches Reisfleisch *diced pork, onions, tomatoes, and rice*
Soleier *pickled eggs*
Soße *sauce, gravy*
Soufflé *soufflé*
Spanferkel *suckling pig*
Spargel *asparagus*
Spätzle *homemade noodles*
Speck *fatty bacon*
Speisekarte *menu*
Spezialität des Hauses *house specialty*
Spiegeleier *fried eggs*
Spießbraten *joint roasted on a spit*
Spinat *spinach*
Spitzkohl *white cabbage*
Sprotten *sprats*
Sprudel(wasser) *mineral water*
Stachelbeeren *gooseberries*
Stangen(weiß)brot *French bread*
Steinbutt *turbot*
Steinpilze *cep mushrooms*
Stollen *stollen (Christmas fruit bread)*
Strammer Max *ham and fried egg on bread*
Streuselkuchen *cake with crumble topping*
Sülze *brawn*
Suppen *soups*
Suppengrün *mixed herbs and vegetables (used in soup)*
süß *sweet*
süß-sauer *sweet-and-sour*
Süßspeisen *sweet dishes*
Süßwasserfische *freshwater fish*
Szegediner Gulasch *goulash with pickled cabbage*

T

Tafelwasser *(still) mineral water*
Tafelwein *table wine*
Tagesgericht *dish of the day*
Tageskarte *menu of the day*
Tagessuppe *soup of the day*
Tatar *steak tartare*
Taube *pigeon*
Tee *tea*
Teigmantel *pastry case*
Thunfisch *tuna*
Tintenfisch *squid*
Tomaten *tomatoes*
Törtchen *tart(s)*
Torte *cake*
Truthahn *turkey*

U, V

überbacken *au gratin*
Ungarischer Gulasch *Hungarian goulash*
ungebraten *not fried*
Vanille *vanilla*
Vanillesoße *vanilla sauce*
verlorene Eier *poached eggs*
Vollkornbrot *dark whole grain bread*
vom Grill *grilled*
vom Kalb *veal*
vom Rind *beef*
vom Rost *grilled*
vom Schwein *pork*
Vorspeisen *hors d'oeuvres, appetizers*

W

Waffeln *waffles*
Waldorfsalat *Waldorf salad (salad with celery, apples, and walnuts)*
Wasser *water*
Wassermelone *watermelon*
Weichkäse *soft cheese*
Weinbergschnecken *snails*
Weinbrand *brandy*
Weincreme *pudding with wine*
Weinschaumcreme *creamed pudding with wine*
Weinsoße *wine sauce*
Weintrauben *grapes*
Weißbier *wheat beer*
Weißbrot *white bread*
Weißkohl *white cabbage*
Weißkraut *white cabbage*
Weißwein *white wine*
Weißwurst *veal sausage*
Weizenbier *fizzy, light-colored beer made with wheat*
Wiener Schnitzel *veal in breadcrumbs*
Wild *game*
Wildschweinkeule *haunch of wild boar*
Wildschweinsteak *wild boar steak*
Windbeutel *cream puff*
Wirsing *savoy cabbage*
Wurst *sausage*
Würstchen *frankfurter(s)*
Wurstplatte *selection of sausages*
Wurstsalat *sausage salad*
Wurstsülze *sausage brawn*
würzig *spicy*

Z

Zander *pike-perch, zander*
Zigeunerschnitzel *veal with peppers and relishes*
Zitrone *lemon*
Zitronencreme *lemon cream*
Zucchini *zucchini*
Zucker *sugar*
Zuckererbsen *snow peas*
Zunge *tongue*
Zungenragout *tongue ragoût*
Zutaten *ingredients*
Zwiebeln *onions*
Zwiebelringe *onion rings*
Zwiebelsuppe *onion soup*
Zwiebeltorte *onion tart*
Zwischengerichte *entrées*

Dictionary
English to German

In German, the gender of a noun is indicated by the word for *the*: **der** for a masculine noun, **die** for feminine, and **das** for neuter. **Die** is also used with plural nouns, and the abbreviations "(m pl)," "(f pl)," and "(nt pl)" are used to indicate their gender here. The feminine form of most occupations and personal attributes is made by adding -in to the masculine form: accountant **Buchhalter(in)**, for example. Exceptions to this rule are listed separately. Where necessary, adjectives are denoted by the abbreviation "(adj)."

A

about: about 16 etwa 16
accelerator das Gaspedal
accident der Unfall
accommodation die Unterkunft
accountant der/die Buchhalter(in)
ache der Schmerz
across from: across from the hotel gegenüber dem Hotel
adapter der Adapter
address die Adresse
admission charge der Eintrittspreis
after nach
aftershave das Rasierwasser
again nochmal
against gegen
agenda die Tagesordnung
agent der Vertreter
air die Luft
air conditioning die Klimaanlage
aircraft das Flugzeug
airline die Fluglinie
airmail die Luftpost
air mattress die Luftmatratze
airport der Flughafen
airport bus der Flughafenbus
aisle der Gang
alarm clock der Wecker
alcohol der Alkohol
all alle(s); *all the streets* alle Straßen; *that's all* das ist alles
allergic allergisch
almost fast
alone allein
already schon
always immer
am: I am ich bin
ambulance der Krankenwagen

America Amerika
American der/die Amerikaner(in); (adj) amerikanisch
and und
ankle der Knöchel
another (different) ein anderer; *(one more)* noch ein; *another time* ein andermal; *another room* ein anderes Zimmer; *another coffee, please* noch einen Kaffee, bitte
answering machine der Anrufbeanworter
antique shop das Antiquitätengeschäft
antiseptic das Antiseptikum
apartment die Wohnung
aperitif der Aperitif
appetite der Appetit
appetizer die Vorspeisen (f pl)
apple der Apfel
application form das Antragsformular
appointment der Termin
apricot die Aprikose
are: you are (singular informal) du bist; *(singular formal; plural formal)* Sie sind; *(plural informal)* ihr seit; *we are* wir sind; *they are* sie sind
arm der Arm
armchair der Sessel
arrivals die Ankunft
art die Kunst
art gallery die Kunstgalerie
artist der/die Künstler(in)
as: as soon as possible so bald wie möglich
ashtray der Aschenbecher
asthma das Asthma
at: at the post office auf der Post; *at the station* am Bahnhof; *at night*

in der Nacht; at 3 o'clock um 3 Uhr
athletic shoes die Turnschuhe
ATM der Geldautomat
attic der Dachboden
attractive attraktiv
August August
aunt die Tante
Australia Australien
Australian der/die Australier(in); (adj) australisch
Austria Österreich
Austrian der/die Österreicher(in); (adj) österreichisch
automatic automatisch
away: is it far away? ist es weit von hier?; *go away!* gehen Sie weg!
awful furchtbar

B

baby das Baby
back (not front) die Rückseite; *(part of body)* der Rücken
backpack der Rucksack
bacon der Speck; *bacon and eggs* Eier mit Speck
bad schlecht
bag die Tasche
baggage das Gepäck; *baggage claim* die Gepäckausgabe
bait der Köder
bake backen
baker der Bäcker
bakery die Konditorei
balcony der Balkon
ball der Ball
ballet das Ballett
Baltic die Ostsee
banana die Banane
band (musicians) die Band
bandage der Verband; *(adhesive)* das Pflaster

bank die Bank

banknote der (Geld)schein

bar (drinks) die Bar

barbecue der Grill

barber's der Herrenfriseur

bargain das Sonderangebot

basement das Untergeschoss

basin (sink) das Becken

basket der Korb

bath das Bad; (tub) die Badewanne; *to have a bath* ein Bad nehmen

bathroom das Badezimmer

bathroom sink das Waschbecken

bathtub die Badewanne

battery die Batterie

Bavaria Bayern

beach der Strand

beans die Bohnen

beard der Bart

beautiful schön

because weil

bed das Bett; *bed linen* die Bettwäsche

bedroom das Schlafzimmer

bedspread die Tagesdecke

beef das Rindfleisch

beer das Bier

before ... vor ...

beginner der Anfänger

behind ... hinter ...

beige beige

Belgian der/die Belgier(in); (adj) belgisch

Belgium Belgien

bell (church) die Glocke; (door) die Klingel

below ... unter ...

belt der Gürtel

beside neben

best bester

better besser

between ... zwischen ...

bicycle das Fahrrad

big groß

bikini der Bikini

bill die Rechnung

biochemistry die Biochemie

bird der Vogel

birthday der Geburtstag; *happy birthday!* Herzlichen Glückwunsch!

birthday card die Geburtstagskarte

birthday present das Geburtstagsgeschenk

bite (by dog) der Biss; (by insect) der Stich; (verb: by dog) beißen; (by insect) stechen

bitter bitter

black schwarz

blackberry die Brombeere

black currant die schwarze Johannisbeere

Black Forest der Schwarzwald

blanket die Decke

bleach das Bleichmittel; (verb: hair) bleichen

blind (unsighted) blind

blinds die Jalousie

blister die Blase

blond (adj) blond

blood das Blut; *blood test* die Blutprobe

blouse die Bluse

blue blau

boarding pass die Bordkarte

boat das Schiff; (small) das Boot

body der Körper; (corpse) die Leiche

boil (verb) kochen

boiled gekocht

boiler der Boiler

bolt (on door) der Riegel; (verb) verriegeln

bone der Knochen

book das Buch; (verb) buchen

bookstore die Buchhandlung

boot der Stiefel

border die Grenze

boring langweilig

*born: I was born in ...*ich bin in ... geboren

both beide; *both of us* wir beide; *both ... and ...* sowohl ... als auch ...

bottle die Flasche

bottle opener der Flaschenöffner

bottom der Boden; (sea) der Grund

bowl die Schüssel

box die Schachtel

boxing das Boxen

box office die Kasse

boy der Junge

boyfriend der Freund

bra der Büstenhalter

bracelet das Armband

brake die Bremse; (verb) bremsen

branch die Zweigstelle

brandy der Weinbrand

bread das Brot

bread shop die Bäckerei

breakdown (car) die Panne

breakfast das Frühstück

breathe atmen

bridge die Brücke; (game) das Bridge

briefcase die Aktentasche

Britain Großbritannien

British britisch

brochure die Broschüre

broken (arm, etc.) gebrochen; (vase, etc.) zerbrochen; (machine, etc.) kaputt; *broken leg* der Beinbruch

brooch die Brosche

brother der Bruder

brother-in-law der Schwager

brown braun

bruise der blaue Fleck

brush die Bürste; (paint) der Pinsel; (verb: hair) bürsten; (floor) kehren

Brussels Brüssel

bucket der Eimer

budget das Budget

builder der/die Bauarbeiter(in)

building das Gebäude

bumper die Stoßstange

burglar der Einbrecher

burn die Verbrennung; (verb) brennen

bus der Bus; (long distance) der Überlandbus, der Reisebus *bus station* der Busbahnhof

business das Geschäft; *it's none of your business* das geht Sie nichts an

business card die Visitenkarte

busy (occupied) beschäftigt; (bar, etc.) voll

but aber

butcher's die Metzgerei

butter die Butter

buy kaufen

by: by the window am Fenster; *by Friday* bis Freitag

C

cabbage der Kohl

cable car die Drahtseilbahn

café das Café

cage der Käfig

cake der Kuchen

calculator der Rechner

call: what's it called? wie heißt das?

camera die Kamera

camper der Wohnwagen

camper van das Wohnmobil

campfire das Lagerfeuer

camping gas das Campinggas

campground der Campingplatz; *campground office* die Campingplatzverwaltung camshaft die Nockenwelle

can (vessel) die Dose; (verb: to be able) can I have ...? kann ich ... haben?; can you ...? können Sie ...?

Canada Kanada

Canadian der/die Kanadier(in); (adj) kanadisch

canal der Kanal

candle die Kerze

canoe das Kanu

can opener der Dosenöffner

cap (bottle) der Verschluss; (hat) die Mütze

car das Auto

carburetor der Vergaser

card die Karte

careful sorgfältig; be careful! passen Sie auf!

caretaker der/die Hausmeister(in)

carpenter der/die Schreiner(in)

carpet der Teppich

car (train) der Wagen

car repairs die Werkstatt

carrot die Möhre, die Karotte

carry-on luggage das Handgepäckcase (suitcase) der Koffer

carry-out (food) der Schnellimbiss

car seat (for baby) der Kindersitz

cart der Kofferkuli

cash das Bargeld; (verb) einlösen; to pay cash bar bezahlen

cashier der/die Kassierer(in)

cassette die Kassette; cassette player der Kassettenrecorder

castle das Schloss, die Burg

cat die Katze

cathedral der Dom

cauliflower der Blumenkohl

cave die Höhle

CD die Compact-Disc, die CD

ceiling die Decke

cellar der Keller

cell phone das Handy, das Mobiltelefon

cemetery der Friedhof

central heating die Zentralheizung

center (middle) die Mitte

certificate die Bescheinigung

chair der Stuhl

change (money) das Kleingeld; (verb: money) wechseln; (clothes) sich umziehen

Channel der Kanal; Channel Tunnel der Kanaltunnel

charger das Ladegerät

cheap billig

check der Scheck; debit card die Scheckkarte; checkbook das Scheckheft

checkout die Kasse

cheers! prost!

cheese der Käse

cherry die Kirsche

chess Schach

chest (part of body) die Brust; (furniture) die Truhe

chest of drawers die Kommode

chewing gum der Kaugummi

chicken das Huhn; (cooked) das Hähnchen

child das Kind

children die Kinder (nt pl)

children's ward die Kinderstation

chimney der Schornstein

china das Porzellan

chips die Chips

chocolate die Schokolade; box of chocolates die Schachtel Pralinen

chop (food) das Kotelett; (verb: to cut) kleinschneiden

Christmas Weihnachten

church die Kirche

cigar die Zigarre; (thin) das Zigarillo

cigarette die Zigarette

circle der Rang

city die (Groß)stadt

class die Klasse

classical music die klassische Musik

clean (adj) sauber

cleaner die Putzfrau

clear klar

clever klug

client der Kunde

clock die Uhr

close (near) nah; (stuffy) stickig; (verb) schließen

closed geschlossen

clothes die Kleider (nt pl)

club der Klub

clubs (cards) Kreuz

clutch die Kupplung

coat der Mantel

coat hanger der (Kleider)bügel

coffee der Kaffee; black coffee der Kaffee ohne Milch

coin die Münze

cold (illness) die Erkältung; (adj) kalt; I have a cold ich bin erkältet; I am cold mir ist kalt

collar das Halsband, der Kragen

collection (stamps, etc.) die Sammlung;

Cologne Köln

color die Farbe; color film der Farbfilm

comb der Kamm

come kommen; I come from ... ich komme aus ...; come here! kommen Sie her! come back zurückkommen

comforter die Steppdecke

compartment das Abteil

complicated kompliziert

computer der Computer; computer games die Computerspiele (nt pl)

concert das Konzert

conditioner (hair) die Haarspülung

condom das Kondom

conductor (bus) der Schaffner; (orchestra) der Dirigent

conference die Konferenz; conference room das Konferenzzimmer

congratulations! herzlichen Glückwunsch!

consulate das Konsulat

consultant der/die Berater(in)

contact lenses die Kontaktlinsen

contraceptive das Verhütungsmittel

contract der Vertrag

cook der Koch; (verb) kochen

cookie das Plätzchen

cool kühl

cork der Korken

corkscrew der Korkenzieher

corner die Ecke

corridor der Korridor

cosmetics die Kosmetika

cost (verb) kosten; what does it cost? was kostet das?

cotton die Baumwolle

cotton balls die Watte

cough der Husten; (verb) husten
countertop die Arbeitsfläche
country das Land
cousin (male) der Vetter; (female) die Kusine
crab die Krabbe
cramp der Krampf
crayfish der Krebs
cream (for cake, etc.) die Sahne; (lotion) die Creme
credit card die Kreditkarte
crib das Kinderbett
crowded überfüllt
cruise die Kreuzfahrt
crutches die Krücken (f pl)
cry (weep) weinen; (shout) rufen
cucumber die Gurke
cufflinks die Manschettenknöpfe (m pl)
cup die Tasse
cupboard der Schrank
curls die Locken (f pl)
curry das Curry
curtain der Vorhang
cushion das Kissen
Customs der Zoll
cut der Schnitt; (verb) schneiden
cycling das Radfahren

D

dad der Papa
dairy products die Molkereiprodukte (nt pl)
damp feucht
dance der Tanz; (verb) tanzen
Dane (man) der Däne; (woman) die Dänin
dangerous gefährlich
Danish dänisch
Danish pastry das Teilchen
Danube die Donau
dark dunkel
daughter die Tochter
day der Tag
dead tot
deaf taub
dear (person) lieb
December Dezember
deck chair der Liegestuhl
deck of cards das Kartenspiel
decorator der/die Maler(in)
deep tief
delayed verspätet
delegate der/die Delegierte(r)
deliberately absichtlich
delicatessen das Feinkostgeschäft
delivery die Lieferung

Denmark Dänemark
dentist der Zahnarzt
dentures die Prothese, das Gebiss
deny bestreiten
deodorant das Deodorant
department store das Kaufhaus
department die Abteilung
departure die Abfahrt
departure lounge die Abflughalle
departures der Abflug
deposit die Kaution
designer der/die Grafiker(in)
desserts der Nachtisch
develop (film) entwickeln
diabetic der/die Diabetiker(in)
diamond (gem) der Diamant
diamonds (cards) Karo
diaper die Windel
diarrhea der Durchfall
planner (calendar) das Tagebuch
dictionary das Wörterbuch
die sterben
diesel der Diesel
different verschieden; *that's different!* das ist etwas anderes!; *I'd like a different kind* ich möchte gern eine andere Sorte
difficult schwierig
dining room der Speiseraum
dinner das Abendessen
directory (telephone) das Telefonbuch
dirty schmutzig
disabled behindert
discounts die Ermäßigungen
dish towel das Geschirrtuch
dishwasher die Geschirrspülmaschine
dishwashing liquid das Spülmittel
disposable diapers die Einwegwindeln
dive der Sprung; (verb) tauchen
diving board das Sprungbett
divorced geschieden
do tun; *how do you do?* guten Tag; (on being introduced) freut mich
doctor der Arzt
document das Dokument
dog der Hund
doll die Puppe
dollar der Dollar
door die Tür

double room das Doppelzimmer
doughnut der Berliner
down herunter; (position) unten; *down here* hier unten
downtown das Stadtzentrum
drawer die Schublade
drawing pin die Heftzwecke, der Reißnagel
dress das Kleid
drink das Getränk; (verb) trinken; *would you like a drink?* möchten Sie etwas trinken?
drinking water das Trinkwasser
drive (verb) fahren
driver der/die Fahrer(in)
driver's license der Führerschein
driveway die Einfahrt
drops die Tropfen
drunk betrunken
dry trocken
dry cleaner die Reinigung
during während
duster das Staubtuch
Dutch (adj) holländisch
Dutchman/woman der/die Holländer(in)
duty-free zollfrei

E

each (every) jeder, alle; *five euros each* fünf Euro das Stück
ear das Ohr; *ears* die Ohren (nt pl)
early früh
earrings die Ohrringe (m pl)
east der Osten
easy leicht
eat essen
egg das Ei
eight acht
eighteen achtzehn
eighty achtzig
either: *either of them* einer von beiden; *either ... or ...* entweder ... oder ...
elastic elastisch; *elastic band* das Gummiband
elbow der Ellbogen
electric elektrisch
electrical hookup der Stromanschluss
electrician der/die Elektriker(in)
electricity der Strom
elevator der Fahrstuhl
eleven elf
else: *something else* etwas anderes;

someone else jemand anders; *somewhere else* woanders
email die Mail
email address die Mail Adresse
embarrassing peinlich
embassy die Botschaft
emerald der Smaragd
emergency der Notfall
emergency brake die Notbremse
emergency department die Unfallstation
emergency exit der Notausgang
empty leer
end das Ende
engaged (couple) verlobt; (occupied) besetzt
engine (motor) der Motor
engineering die Technik
England England
English (adj) englisch; (language) Englisch
Englishman/woman der/die Engländer(in)
enlargement die Vergrößerung
enough genug
entertainment die Unterhaltung
entrance der Eingang; *entrance ticket* die Eintrittskarte
envelope der (Brief)umschlag
epileptic der/die Epileptiker(in)
escalator die Rolltreppe
especially besonders
estimate der Kostenvoranschlag
evening der Abend
every jeder
everyone jeder
everything alles
everywhere überall
example das Beispiel; *for example* zum Beispiel
excellent ausgezeichnet
excess baggage das Mehrgepäck
exchange (verb) (um)tauschen
exchange rate der Wechselkurs
excursion der Ausflug
excuse me! Entschuldigung!
executive der/die Manager(in)
exhaust der Auspuff
exhibition die Ausstellung
exit der Ausgang
expensive teuer

expressway die Autobahn
extension cord die Verlängerungsschnur
eye das Auge; *eyes* die Augen
eyebrow das Augenbraue

F

face das Gesicht
faint (unclear) blass; (verb) ohnmächtig werden
fair (funfair) der Jahrmarkt, die Kirmes; (just) gerecht, fair
false teeth die Prothese, das Gebiss
family die Familie
fan (ventilator) der Ventilator; (enthusiast) der Fan
fan belt der Keilriemen
fantastic fantastisch
far weit; *how far is it?* wie weit ist es?
fare der Fahrpreis
farm der Bauernhof
farmer der Bauer
fashion die Mode
fast schnell
fat das Fett; (person) dick
father der Vater
fax das Fax; (verb) faxen; *fax machine* das Faxgerät
February Februar
feel (touch) fühlen; *I feel hot* mir ist heiß; *I feel like ...* ich möchte gern ...; *I don't feel well* mir ist nicht gut
feet die Füße (m pl)
fence der Zaun
ferry die Fähre
fever das Fieber
fiancé der Verlobte
fiancée die Verlobte
field das Feld; (of work) das Gebiet
fifteen fünfzehn
fifty fünfzig
fig die Feige
filling (in tooth, cake) die Füllung; (in sandwich) der Belag
film der Film
filter der Filter
filter papers das Filterpapier
finger der Finger
fire das Feuer
fire extinguisher der Feuerlöscher
fireworks das Feuerwerk
first erster; *first class* erster Klasse
first aid die Erste Hilfe

first floor der erste Stock
first name der Vorname
fish der Fisch
fishing das Angeln; *to go fishing* Angeln gehen
fishmonger das Fischgeschäft
five fünf
fizzy sprudelnd
flag die Fahne
flash (camera) der Blitz
flashlight die Taschenlampe
flat (level) flach; (apartment) die Wohnung
flat tire der Platten
flavor der Geschmack
flea der Floh
flea spray das Flohspray
flight der Flug; *flight number* die Flugnummer
flippers die (Schwimm)flossen (f pl)
floor (ground) der Fußboden, der Boden; (story) der Stock
florist der Blumenladen
flour das Mehl
flower die Blume; *flower-arranging* das Blumenstecken; *flowerbed* das Blumenbeet
flute die Flöte
fly (insect) die Fliege; (verb) fliegen
flysheet das Überzelt
fog der Nebel
folk music die Volksmusik
food das Essen
food poisoning die Lebensmittelvergiftung
foot der Fuß
for für; *for me* für mich; *what for?* wofür?; *for a week* für eine Woche
foreigner der/die Ausländer(in)
forest der Wald
forget vergessen
fork die Gabel
forty vierzig
fountain der Brunnen
four vier
fourteen vierzehn
fourth vierter
France Frankreich
free frei; (no charge) kostenlos, gratis
freezer der Gefrierschrank
French französisch
french fries die Fritten, die Pommes (m pl)
Frenchman der Franzose
Frenchwoman die Französin

Friday Freitag
fried gebraten
friend der/die Freund(in)
friendly freundlich
front: in front of ... vor ...
frost der Frost
frozen foods die Tiefkühlkost
fruit das Obst, die Frucht
fruit juice der Fruchtsaft
fry braten
frying pan die (Brat)pfanne
full voll; *I'm full (up)* ich bin satt
full board Vollpension
funny komisch
furniture die Möbel

G

garage die Garage; (for repairs) die Werkstatt
garbage der Abfall
garbage bag der Müllsack
garden der Garten
garden center das Gartencenter
gardener der/die Gärtner(in)
gardening die Gartenarbeit
garlic der Knoblauch
gasoline das Benzin
gas station die Tankstelle
gate das Tor; (garden gate) die Pforte; (at airport) der Flugsteig
gay (homosexual) schwul
gear der Gang
gearbox das Getriebe
gearshift der Schaltknüppel
gel (hair) das Gel
German der/die Deutsche; (adj) deutsch; (language) Deutsch
Germany Deutschland
get (fetch) holen; *have you got ...?* haben Sie ...?; *to get the train* den Zug nehmen
get back: we get back tomorrow wir kommen morgen zurück; *to get something back* etwas zurückbekommen
get in hereinkommen; (arrive) ankommen
get off (bus, etc.) aussteigen
get on (bus, etc.) einsteigen
get out herauskommen; (bring out) herausholen
get up (rise) aufstehen

gift das Geschenk
gin der Gin
ginger (spice) der Ingwer
girl das Mädchen
girlfriend die Freundin
give geben
glad froh
glass das Glas
glasses die Brille
gloves die Handschuhe
glue der Leim, der Klebstoff
go gehen; (travel) fahren; (by plane) fliegen
gold das Gold
good gut
goodbye Auf Wiedersehen
good night Guten Abend
government die Regierung
granddaughter die Enkelin
grandfather der Großvater
grandmother die Großmutter
grandparents die Großeltern (m pl)
grandson der Enkel
grapes die Trauben (f pl)
grass das Gras
gray grau
Great Britain Großbritannien
great: great! prima!
green grün
grill der Grill
grilled gegrillt
grocery store das Lebensmittelgeschäft
ground floor das Erdgeschoss
groundsheet der Zeltboden
guarantee die Garantie; (verb) garantieren
guard der Wächter
guest der Gast
guide der Führer
guidebook der (Reise)führer
guided tour die Führung
guitar die Gitarre
gun (rifle) das Gewehr
gutter die Dachrinne
gym das Sportzentrum

H

hair das Haar
haircut der Haarschnitt
hairdresser's der Friseur; (ladies') der Friseursalon
hair dryer der Fön
hair spray das Haarspray
half halb; *half an hour* eine halbe Stunde
half-board Halbpension

half-brother der Halbbruder
half-sister die Halbschwester
ham der gekochte Schinken
hamburger der Hamburger
hammer der Hammer
hamster der Hamster
hand die Hand
handbag die Handtasche
handbrake die Handbremse
handle (door) die Klinke
handshake der Händedruck
handsome gut aussehend
hangover der Kater
happy glücklich
harbor der Hafen
hard hart; (difficult) schwer
hardware store der Eisenwarenhändler
hat der Hut
have (verb) haben: *I have* ich habe; *you have* (singular informal) du hast; (plural informal) ihr habt; (singular formal; plural formal) Sie haben; *we have* wir haben; *they have* sie haben; *do you have ...?* haben Sie ...?; *I have to go* ich muss gehen
hay fever der Heuschnupfen
he er
head der Kopf
headache die Kopfschmerzen
headlights die Scheinwerfer
headphones der Kopfhörer
headquarters die Zentrale
hear hören
hearing aid das Hörgerät
heart das Herz
heart condition: I have a heart condition Ich bin herzkrank
hearts (cards) Herz
heater das Heizgerät
heating die Heizung
heavy schwer
hedge die Hecke
heel (shoe) der Absatz; (foot) die Ferse
hello guten Tag; (on phone) hallo
help die Hilfe; (verb) helfen

her: it's her sie ist es; *it's for her* es ist für sie; *give it to her* geben Sie es ihr; *her book* ihr Buch; *her shoes* ihre Schuhe; *it's hers* es gehört ihr
hi hallo
high hoch
hiking das Wandern
hill der Berg
him: it's him er ist es; *it's for him* es ist für ihn; *give it to him* geben Sie es ihm
hire leihen, mieten
his: his book sein Buch; *his shoes* seine Schuhe; *it's his* es gehört ihm
history die Geschichte
hitchhike trampen
HIV-positive HIV positiv
hobby das Hobby
holiday die Ferien
Holland Holland
home: at home zu Hause
home improvement das Basteln
homeopathy die Homöopathie
honest ehrlich
honey der Honig
honeymoon die Hochzeitsreise
hood (car) die Motorhaube
horn (car) die Hupe; (animal) das Horn
horrible schrecklich
hospital das Krankenhaus
host der/die Gastgeber(in)
hour die Stunde
house das Haus
household products die Haushaltswaren (f pl)
how? wie?
humanities die Geisteswissenschaften (f pl)
hundred hundert
hungry: I'm hungry ich habe Hunger
hurry: I'm in a hurry ich bin in Eile
husband der (Ehe)mann

I

I ich
ice das Eis
ice cream das Eis, die Eiscreme
ice pop das Eis am Stiel
ice skates die Schlittschuhe
ice-skating: to go ice-skating Schlittschuh laufen gehen
if wenn
ignition die Zündung

ill krank
immediately sofort
impossible unmöglich
in in; *in English* auf Englisch; *in the hotel* im Hotel
indigestion die Magenverstimmung
infection die Infektion, die Entzündung
information die Information
injection die Spritze
injury die Verletzung
ink die Tinte
inn das Gasthaus
inner tube der Schlauch
insect das Insekt
insect repellent das Insektenmittel
insomnia die Schlaflosigkeit
instant coffee der Pulverkaffee
insurance die Versicherung
interesting interessant
Internet das Internet
interpret dolmetschen
interpreter der/die Dolmetscher(in)
intravenous drip die intravenöse Infusion
invitation die Einladung
invoice die Rechnung
Ireland Irland
Irish irisch
Irishman der Ire
Irishwoman die Irin
iron (material) das Eisen; (for clothes) das Bügeleisen; (verb) bügeln
is: he/she/it is ... er/sie/es ist ...
island die Insel
it es
Italian der/die Italiener(in); (adj) italienisch
Italy Italien

J

jacket die Jacke
jam die Marmelade, die Konfitüre
January Januar
jazz der Jazz
jeans die Jeans
jellyfish die Qualle
jeweler das Juweliergeschäft
jewelry der Schmuck
job die Arbeit
jog (verb) joggen; *to go for a jog* joggen gehen
jogging suit der Trainingsanzug

joke der Witz
journey die Fahrt, die Reise
July Juli
jumper der Pullover
June Juni
just (only) nur; *it's just arrived* es ist gerade angekommen

K

kerosene das Paraffin
key der Schlüssel
keyboard die Tastatur
kidney die Niere
kilo das Kilo
kilometer der Kilometer
kitchen die Küche
knee das Knie
knife das Messer
knit stricken
knitwear die Strickwaren (f pl)
know wissen; (be acquainted with) kennen; *I don't know* ich weiß nicht

L

label das Etikett
lace die Spitze
laces (shoe) die Schnürsenkel (m pl)
ladies' room die Damentoilette
lady die Dame
lake der See
lamb (animal) das Lamm; (meat) das Lammfleisch
lamp die Lampe
lampshade der Lampenschirm
land das Land; (verb) landen
language die Sprache
laptop der Laptop
large groß
last (final) letzter; *last week* letzte Woche; *at last!* endlich!
last name der Nachname
late spät; *the bus is late* der Bus hat Verspätung
later später
laugh lachen
laundromat der Waschsalon
laundry (place) die Wäscherei; (dirty clothes) die Wäsche
laundry detergent das Waschpulver
lawn der Rasen
lawnmower der Rasenmäher

lawyer der Rechtsanwalt/die Rechtsanwältin

laxative das Abführmittel

lazy faul

lead die Leine

leaf das Blatt

leaflet die Broschüre, der Flyer

learn lernen

leather das Leder

lecture hall der Vorlesungssaal

leeks das Breitlauch, der Porrée

left (not right) links; *there's nothing left* es ist nichts mehr übrig

left luggage locker das Gepäckschließfach

left side die linke Seite

leg das Bein

lemon die Zitrone

lemon soda die Limonade

length die Länge

lens die Linse

less weniger

lesson die Stunde

letter (post) der Brief; (alphabet) der Buchstabe

lettuce der Kopfsalat

library die Bibliothek, die Bücherei

license die Genehmigung; (driver's) der Führerschein

license plate das Nummernschild

life das Leben

lift: could you give me a lift? können Sie mich mitnehmen?

light das Licht; (adj) leicht; (not dark) hell

light bulb die (Glüh)birne

lighter das Feuerzeug; *lighter fuel* das Feuerzeugbenzin

light meter der Belichtungsmesser

like: I like you ich mag Sie; *I like swimming* ich schwimme gern; *it's like ...* es ist wie ...; *like this* so

lime (fruit) die Limette

line (waiting) die Schlange; *line up* anstehen

lip balm der Lippen-Fettstift

lipstick der Lippenstift

liqueur der Likör

list die Liste

liter der Liter

litter der Abfall

little (small) klein; *it's a little big* es ist ein bisschen zu groß; *just a little* nur ein bisschen

liver die Leber

lobster der Hummer

lollipop der Lutscher

long lang

lost property das Fundbüro

lot: a lot viel

loud laut; (color) grell

lounge das Wohnzimmer; (in hotel) die Lounge

love die Liebe; (verb) lieben

low niedrig; (voice) tief

luck das Glück; *good luck!* viel Glück!

luggage der Koffer, das Gepäck; *luggage rack* die Gepäckablage

lunch das Mittagessen

Luxembourg Luxemburg

M

mad verrückt

magazine die Zeitschrift

maid das Zimmermädchen

mail die Post

mail die Post; (verb) aufgeben

mailbox der Briefkasten

mail carrier der/die Briefträger(in)

main courses die Hauptgerichte

main road die Hauptstraße

make machen

makeup das Make-up

man der Mann

manager der Geschäftsführer

many: not many nicht viele

map (of country) die Landkarte; (of town) der Stadtplan

marble der Marmor

March März

margarine die Margarine

market der Markt

marmalade die Orangenmarmelade

married verheiratet

mascara das Maskara, die Wimperntusche

mass (church) die Messe

match (light) das Streichholz; (sport) das Spiel

material (fabric) der Stoff

matter: it doesn't matter das macht nichts

mattress die Matratze

maybe vielleicht

me: it's me ich bin's; *it's for me* es ist für mich; *give it to me* geben Sie es mir

meal das Essen

mean: what does this mean? was bedeutet das?

meat das Fleisch

mechanic der/die Mechaniker(in)

medication die Medikamente

medicine die Medizin

meeting die Besprechung, das Treffen

melon die Melone

men's room die Herrentoilette

menu die Speisekarte

message die Nachricht

metro station die U-Bahnstation

microwave die Mikrowelle

middle: in the middle in der Mitte

midnight Mitternacht

milk die Milch

mine: it's mine es gehört mir

mineral water das Mineralwasser

minute die Minute

mirror der Spiegel

Miss Fräulein

mistake der Fehler

modem das Modem

modern architecture die moderne Architektur

mom die Mama

Monday Montag

money das Geld

monitor der Monitor, der Bildschirm

month der Monat

monument das Denkmal

moon der Mond

moped das Moped

more mehr

morning der Morgen; *in the morning* am Morgen

mother die Mutter

motorbike das Motorrad

motorboat das Motorboot

mountain der Berg

mountain bike das Mountain-Bike

mouse die Maus

mousse (for hair) der Schaumfestiger

mouth der Mund

move (verb) bewegen; (house) umziehen; *don't move!* stillhalten!

movie der Film

movie theater das Kino

Mr. Herr

Mrs. Frau
Ms. Frau
much viel
Munich München
museum das Museum
mushroom der Pilz
music die Musik
musical instrument das Musikinstrument
musician der/die Musiker(in)
mussels die Muscheln (f pl)
must: I must ... ich muss ...
mustache der Schnurrbart
mustard der Senf
my: my book mein Buch; *my keys* meine Schlüssel

N

nail (metal, finger) der Nagel
nail clippers der Nagelzwicker
nailfile die Nagelfeile
nail polish der Nagellack
name der Name; *what's your name?* wie heißen Sie?
napkin die Serviette
near nah; *near the door* nahe der Tür; *near London* in der Nähe von London
necessary notwendig
neck der Hals
necklace die Halskette
need (verb) brauchen; *I need ...* ich brauche ...; *there's no need* das ist nicht nötig
needle die Nadel
negative (photo) das Negativ
nephew der Neffe
Netherlands die Niederlande
never nie
new neu
news die Nachrichten
newspaper die Zeitung
newsstand der Zeitungsladen
New Zealand Neuseeland
New Zealander der/die Neuseeländer(in)
next nächster; *next week* nächste Woche
nice (attractive) hübsch; (pleasant) angenehm; (to eat) lecker
niece die Nichte
night die Nacht
nightclub der Nachtklub
nightgown das Nachthemd
night porter der Nachtportier
nightstand der Nachttisch
nine neun
nineteen neunzehn
ninety neunzig
no (response) nein; *I have no money* ich habe kein Geld
noisy laut
noon der Mittag
north der Norden
Northern Ireland Nordirland
North Sea die Nordsee
nose die Nase
not nicht
notebook das Notizbuch
notepad der Notizblock
notes die Banknoten (f pl)
nothing nichts
novel der Roman
November November
now jetzt
nowhere nirgendwo
number die Zahl; (telephone) die Nummer
nurse (man) der Krankenpfleger; (woman) die Krankenschwester
nut (fruit) die Nuss; (for bolt) die Mutter

O

occasionally gelegentlich
October Oktober
of von; *the name of the hotel* der Name des Hotels
office das Büro
often oft
oil das Öl
ointment die Salbe
OK okay
old alt; *how old are you?* wie alt sind Sie?
olive die Olive
omelet das Omelette
on ... auf ...
one (number) eins; *one beer/sausage* ein Bier/eine Wurst
one million eine Million
one-way ticket die einfache Fahrkarte
onion die Zwiebel
only nur
open (verb) öffnen; (adj) offen
opening times die Öffnungszeiten
opera die Oper
operating room der Operationssaal
operation die Operation
operator die Vermittlung
optician Augenarzt/ Augenärztin
or oder
orange (color) orange; (fruit) die Orange
orange juice der Orangensaft
orchestra das Orchester
ordinary gewöhnlich
other: the other ... der/die/das andere ...
our unser; *it's ours* es gehört uns
out aus; *he's out* er ist nicht da
outside außerhalb
oven der Backofen
over (more than) über; (finished) vorbei; (across) über; *over there* dort drüben
overpass die Überführung
oyster die Auster

P

pacifier (for baby) der Schnuller
package das Paket
pack (cigarettes) die Schachtel
padlock das Vorhängeschloss
page die Seite
pain der Schmerz
painkiller (medicine) die Schmerztablette
paint die Farbe
pair das Paar
pajamas der Schlafanzug
palace der Palast
pale blass
pancake der Pfannkuchen
pants die Hose
pantyhose die Strumpfhose
paper das Papier; (newspaper) die Zeitung
parcel das Paket
pardon? wie bitte?
parents die Eltern (m pl)
park der Park; (verb) parken; *no parking* Parken verboten
parking lot der Parkplatz
parsley die Petersilie
part (hair) der Scheitel
party (celebration) die Party; (group) die Gruppe; (political) die Partei
pass überholen
passenger der Fahrgast, der Passagier
passport der Pass, der Ausweis; *passport control* die Passkontrolle

password das Passwort
pasta die Nudeln
pastry das Gebäck
path der Weg
pay bezahlen
payment die Bezahlung
peach der Pfirsich
peanuts die Erdnüsse (f pl)
pear die Birne
pearl die Perle
peas die Erbsen (f pl)
pedestrian der Fußgänger
pedestrian zone die Fußgängerzone
peg (clothes) der Wäscheklammer; *(tent)* der Hering
pen der Stift
pencil der Bleistift; *pencil sharpener* der Bleistiftspitzer
penicillin das Penizillin
penknife das Taschenmesser
pen-pal der/die Brieffreund(in)
people die Leute (m pl)
pepper der Pfeffer; *(red/green)* der Paprika
peppermints die Pfefferminzbonbons
per: per night pro Nacht
perfect perfekt
perfume das Parfüm
perhaps vielleicht
perm die Dauerwelle
pet passport der Tierpass
pets die Haustiere (nt pl)
pharmacy die Apotheke
phone card die Telefonkarte
photocopier der Fotokopierer
photograph das Foto; *(verb)* fotografieren
photographer der Fotograf
phrasebook der Sprachführer
piano das Klavier
pickpocket der Taschendieb
pickup (postal) die Leerung
picnic das Picknick
piece das Stück
pill die Tablette
pillow das Kopfkissen
pilot der/die Pilot(in)
pin die Stecknadel
PIN (number) die Geheimzahl
pineapple die Ananas
pink rosa
pipe (for smoking) die Pfeife; *(for water)* die Pumpe, das Rohr
piston der Kolben

place der Platz; *(town, etc.)* der Ort; *at your place* bei Ihnen
plant die Pflanze
plastic das Plastik
plastic bag die Tragetasche, die Plastiktüte
plate der Teller
platform das Gleis, der Bahnsteig
play (theater) das Stück; *(verb)* spielen
please bitte
plug (electrical) der Stecker; *(sink)* der Stöpsel
plumber der/die Klempner(in)
pocket die Tasche
poison das Gift
Poland Polen
Pole (man) der Pole; *(woman)* die Polin
police die Polizei
police officer der/die Polizist(in)
police report der Polizeibericht
police station das Polizeirevier
Polish polnisch
politics die Politik
poor arm; *(bad quality)* schlecht
pop music die Popmusik
pork das Schweinefleisch
port (harbor) der Hafen
porter (hotel) der Portier
possible möglich
postcard die Postkarte
poster das Poster
post office das Postamt
potato die Kartoffel
pottery die Töpferei
poultry das Geflügel
pound (money, weight) das Pfund
pram der Kinderwagen
prefer: I prefer … ich mag lieber …
pregnant schwager
prescription das Rezept
presentation der Vortrag
pretty (beautiful) schön; *(quite)* ziemlich; *pretty good* recht gut
price der Preis
priest Geistliche
printer der Drucker
private privat
problem das Problem
professor der/die Professor(in)
profits der Gewinn
public öffentlich
public holiday der Feiertag
pull ziehen
puncture die Reifenpanne
purple lila

purse das Portemonnaie
push drücken
put legen, stellen, setzen

Q

quality die Qualität
quarter das Viertel
quay der Kai
question die Frage
quick schnell
quiet still, ruhig
quite (fairly) ziemlich; *(fully)* ganz

R

rabbit das Kaninchen
radiator der Heizkörper; *(car)* der Kühler
radio das Radio
radish der Rettich; *(small red)* das Radieschen
railroad die Bahn
rain der Regen
raincoat der Regenmantel
raisins die Rosinen (f pl)
rake der Rechen
rare (uncommon) selten; *(steak)* blutig
raspberries die Himbeeren (f pl)
rat die Ratte
razor blades die Rasierklingen (f pl)
read lesen
reading lamp die Leselampe
ready fertig
rear lights die Rücklichter (f pl)
receipt die Quittung
reception der Empfang
receptionist die Empfangsperson
record (music) die Schallplatte; *(sports, etc.)* der Rekord
record store das Schallplattengeschäft
red rot
refreshments die Erfrischungen (f pl)
refrigerator der Kühlschrank
registered mail das Einschreiben
relative der Verwandte
relax sich entspannen
religion die Religion
remember sich erinnern; *I don't remember* ich erinnere mich nicht
rent (verb) mieten
report der Bericht
research die Forschungen
reservation die Reservierung

rest (remainder) der Rest; (verb) sich ausruhen

restaurant das Restaurant

return (come back) zurückkommen; (give back) zurückgeben

rhubarb der Rhabarber

rice der Reis

rich reich

right (correct) richtig; (direction) rechts

right side die rechte Seite

ring (jewelry) der Ring; (verb: to call) anrufen

ripe reif

river der Fluss

road die Straße

roasted geröstet

robbery der Diebstahl

rock (stone) der Stein; (music) der Rock

roll (bread) das Brötchen

roof das Dach

room das Zimmer; (space) der Raum

room service der Zimmerservice

rope das Seil

rose die Rose

round (circular) rund

round-trip ticket die Rückfahrkarte

rubber (eraser) der Radiergummi; (material) der Gummi

ruby (stone) der Rubin

rug (mat) der Läufer; (blanket) die Wolldecke

ruins die Ruinen (f pl)

ruler (for drawing) das Lineal

rum der Rum

run (verb) laufen

runway die Start- und Landebahn

S

sad traurig

safe sicher

safety pin die Sicherheitsnadel

sailboat das Segelboot

sailing das Segeln

salad der Salat

salami die Salami

sale (at lower prices) der Schlussverkauf

sales der Absatz

salmon der Lachs

salt das Salz

same: the same dress das gleiche Kleid; *same again, please* nochmal dasselbe, bitte

sand der Sand

sandals die Sandalen (f pl)

sandwich das Sandwich, das Butterbrot

sanitary napkins die Damenbinden (f pl)

Saturday Samstag

sauce die Soße

saucepan der Kochtopf

saucer die Untertasse

sauna die Sauna

sausage die Wurst

say sagen; *what did you say?* was haben Sie gesagt?; *how do you say …?* wie sagt man …?

Scandinavia Skandinawien

scarf (neck) der Schal; (head) das Kopftuch

schedule der Zeitplan; (train, bus) der Fahrplan

school die Schule

scissors die Schere

Scotland Schottland

Scotsman der Schotte

Scotswoman die Schottin

Scottish schottisch

screen der Bildschirm

screw die Schraube

screwdriver der Schraubenzieher

sea das Meer

seafood die Meeresfrüchte (f pl)

seat der Sitz

seatbelt der Sicherheitsgurt

second (time) die Sekunde; (in series) zweiter; *second class* zweiter Klasse

secretary der/die Sekrätär(in)

see sehen; *I can't see* ich kann nichts sehen; *I see* ich verstehe; *see you soon* bis bald; *see you tomorrow* bis Morgen

self-employed selbständig

sell verkaufen

seminar das Seminar

separate getrennt

separated: we are separated wir leben getrennt

separately getrennt

September September

serious ernst

seven sieben

seventeen siebzehn

seventy siebzig

several mehrere

sew nähen

shampoo das Shampoo

shave: to shave sich rasieren

shaving foam die Rasiercreme

shawl das Umhängetuch

she sie

sheet das (Bett)laken

shell die Muschel

shellfish (as food) die Meeresfrüchte (f pl)

sherry der Sherry

ship das Schiff

shirt das Hemd

shoelaces die Schnürsenkel (m pl)

shoe polish die Schuhcreme

shoe store das Schuhgeschäft

shoes die Schuhe (m pl)

shop das Geschäft

shopkeeper der/die Verkäufer(in)

shopping das Einkaufen; (items bought) die Einkäufe; *to go shopping* einkaufen gehen

short kurz

shorts die Shorts

shoulder die Schulter

shower (bath) die Dusche; (rain) der Schauer

shower gel das Duschgel

shrimp die Krabben (f pl)

shutter (camera) der Verschluss; (window) der Fensterladen

sick (ill) krank; *I feel sick* mir ist übel; *to be sick* (vomit) sich übergeben

side die Seite; (edge) die Kante

sidelights das Standlicht

sidewalk der Bürgersteig

sightseeing die Besichtigungen

sign das Schild

silk die Seide

silver (metal) das Silber; (color) silber

simple einfach

sing singen

singing das Singen

single (one) einziger; (unmarried) ledig, single

single room das Einzelzimmer

sister die Schwester

sister-in-law die Schwägerin

six sechs

sixteen sechzehn

sixty sechzig

ski (verb) Ski fahren

ski binding die Skibindung

ski boots die Skistiefel (m pl)

skid (verb) schleudern

skiing: to go skiing Skifahren gehen

ski lift der Skilift

ski poles die Skistöcke (m pl)

ski resort der Skiurlaubsort

skin cleanser der Hautreiniger

skirt der Rock

skis die Skier (m pl)

sky der Himmel

sled der Schlitten

sleep der Schlaf; (verb) schlafen

sleeping bag der Schlafsack

sleeping pill die Schlaftablette

sleeve der Ärmel

slice of ... das Stück ...

slippers die Pantoffeln (m pl)

slow langsam

small klein

smell der Geruch; (verb) riechen

smile das Lächeln; (verb) lächeln

smoke der Rauch; (verb) rauchen

snack der Imbiss

snow der Schnee

so so; *not so much* nicht so viel

soaking solution (for contact lenses) die Aufbewahrungslösung

soap die Seife

socks die Socken (f pl)

soccer der Fußball

soda water das Sodawasser

sofa die Couch, das Sofa

soft weich

soil die Erde

somebody jemand

somehow irgendwie

something etwas

sometimes manchmal

somewhere irgendwo

son der Sohn

song das Lied

sorry! (apology) Verzeihung!, Entschuldigung!; *I'm sorry* es tut mir Leid

soup die Suppe

south der Süden

South Africa Südafrika

souvenir das Souvenir

spa der Kurort

spade (shovel) der Spaten

spades (cards) Pik

spares die Ersatzteile (nt pl)

spark plug die Zündkerze

sparkling water Wasser mit Kohlensäure, das Sprudelwasser

speak sprechen; *do you speak English?* sprechen Sie Englisch?; *I don't*

speak German ich spreche kein Deutsch

speed die Geschwindigkeit

spider die Spinne

spinach der Spinat

spoon der Löffel

sport der Sport

spring (mechanical) die Feder; (season) der Frühling

square (shape) das Quadrat; (in town) der Platz

stadium das Stadion

staircase die Treppe

stairs die Treppe

stamp die Briefmarke

stand der Stand

stapler der Hefter

star der Stern; (film) der Star

start der Start, der Anfang; (verb) anfangen

statement die Aussage

station der Bahnhof; (underground) die Station

statue die Statue

steak das Steak

steal stehlen; *it's been stolen* es ist gestohlen worden

steamed gedämpft

steamer (boat) der Dampfer; (cooking) der Dampfkochtopf

steering wheel das Lenkrad

stepdaughter der Stieftochter

stepfather der Stiefvater

stepmother der Stiefmutter

stepson der Stiefsohn

stereo system die Musikanlange

still water Wasser ohne Kohlensäure, das Tafelwasser

sting der Stich; (verb) stechen

stockings die Strümpfe (m pl)

stomach der Magen

stomachache die Magenschmerzen

stop (bus stop) die Haltestelle; (verb) anhalten; *stop!* halt!

storm der Sturm

stove der Herd

strawberries die Erdbeeren (f pl)

stream (water) der Bach

street die Straße

string (cord) der Faden; (guitar, etc.) die Saite

stroller der Sportwagen

strong (person, drink)

stark; (material) stabil; (taste) streng

student der/die Student(in)

stupid dumm

suburbs der Stadtrand

subway die U-Bahn

sugar der Zucker

suit der Anzug; *it suits you* es steht Ihnen

suitcase der Koffer

sun die Sonne

sunbathe sonnenbaden

sunburn der Sonnenbrand

Sunday Sonntag

sunglasses die Sonnenbrille

sunny: it's sunny es ist sonnig

sunshade der Sonnenschirm

suntan: to get a suntan braun werden

suntan lotion das Sonnenöl

suntanned braungebrannt

superior Vorgesetzte

supermarket der Supermarkt

supper das Abendessen

supplement der Zuschlag

suppository das Zäpfchen

sure sicher

suspenders die Hosenträger (nt pl)

sweat der Schweiß; (verb) schwitzen

sweatshirt das Sweatshirt

sweet (not sour) süß; (confectionery) die Süßigkeit, der Bonbon

swim (verb) schwimmen

swimming das Schwimmen

swimming pool das Schwimmbad

swimming trunks die Badehose

swimsuit der Badeanzug

Swiss der/die Schweizer(in); (adj) schweizerisch

switch der Schalter

Switzerland die Schweiz

swivel chair der Drehstuhl

synagogue die Synagoge

syringe die Spritze

syrup der Sirup

T

table der Tisch

tablet die Tablette

take nehmen

takeoff der Abflug

talcum powder der Puder

talk das Gespräch; (verb) reden

tall groß

tampons die Tampons (m pl)

tangerine die Mandarine

tap der Hahn

tapestry der Wandteppich

taxi das Taxi

taxi stand der Taxistand

tea der Tee; *black tea* der schwarze Tee; *tea with milk* der Tee mit Milch

teacher der/die Lehrer(in)

teakettle der Wasserkessel

telephone das Telefon; (verb) telefonieren

telephone booth die Telefonzelle

television das Fernsehen; *to watch television* fernsehen

temperature die Temperatur; (fever) das Fieber

ten zehn

tennis das Tennis

tent das Zelt

tent peg der Hering

ten thousand zehntausend

tent pole die Zeltstange

terminal das Terminal

terrace die Terrasse

than: bigger than größer als

thank (verb) danken; *thanks* danke; *thank you* danke schön

that: that man dieser Mann; *that woman* diese Frau; *what's that?* was ist das?; *I think that ...* ich denke, dass ...

the der (masculine singular); die (feminine singular); das (neuter singular); die (plural)

theater das Theater

their: their room ihr Zimmer; *their books* ihre Bücher; *it's theirs* es gehört ihnen

them: it's them sie sind es; *it's for them* es ist für sie; *give it to them* geben Sie es ihnen

then dann

there is/are ... es gibt ...; *is/are there ...?* gibt es ...?

these diese

they sie

thick dick

thief der Dieb

thin dünn

think denken; *I think so* ich glaube ja; *I'll think about it* ich überlege es mir

third dritter

thirsty durstig; *I'm thirsty* ich habe Durst

thirteen dreizehn

thirty Dreißig

this: this man dieser Mann; *this woman* diese Frau; *what's this?* was ist das?; *this is Mr ...* das ist Herr ...

those diese da; *those things* die Dinge dort

thousand tausend

three drei

three hundred dreihundert

throat die Kehle

throat lozenges die Halstabletten (f pl)

through durch

thunderstorm das Gewitter

Thursday Donnerstag

ticket die Karte; *ticket kiosk* der Schalter

tide: high tide die Flut; *low tide* die Ebbe

tie die Krawatte; (verb) festmachen

tight eng

tiles die Kacheln (f pl)

time die Zeit; *what's the time?* wie spät ist es?

tip (money) das Trinkgeld; (end) die Spitze

tire der Reifen

tired müde

tissues die Taschentücher

to: to England nach England; *to the station* zum Bahnhof; *to the doctor* zum Arzt

toast der Toast

tobacco der Tabak

toboggan der Schlitten

today heute

together zusammen

toilet die Toilette

toilet paper das Toilettenpapier

tomato die Tomate

tomato juice der Tomatensaft

tomorrow morgen

tongue die Zunge

tonic das Tonic

tonight heute abend

too (also) auch; (excessively) zu

tooth der Zahn

toothache die Zahnschmerzen

toothbrush die Zahnbürste

toothpaste die Zahnpasta

tour die Rundreise

tour guide der/die Reiseleiter(in)

tourist der/die Tourist(in)

tourist office das Verkehrsbüro, die Fremdenverkehrsbüro

towel das Handtuch

tower der Turm

town die Stadt

town hall das Rathaus

toy das Spielzeug

tractor der Traktor

trade fair die Handelsmesse

tradition die Tradition

traffic der Verkehr

traffic jam der Stau

traffic lights die Ampel

trailer der Anhänger

train der Zug

trainee der/die Auszubildende

tram die Straßenbahn

translate übersetzen

translator der/die Übersetzer(in)

trash can die Mülleimer, die Mülltonne

travel agency das Reisebüro

traveler's check der Reisescheck

tray das Tablett

tree der Baum

truck der Lastwagen

true wahr

trunk (car) der Kofferraum*try* versuchen

Tuesday Dienstag

tunnel der Tunnel

Turk (man) der Türke; (woman) die Türkin

Turkey die Türkei

Turkish türkisch

turn signal; der Blinker

tweezers die Pinzette

twelve zwölf

twenty zwanzig

twin beds die zwei Einzelbetten

two zwei

typewriter die Schreibmaschine

U

ugly hässlich

umbrella der (Regen)schirm

uncle der Onkel

under ... unter ...

underpants die Unterhose

underskirt der Unterrock

understand verstehen; *I don't understand* ich verstehe nicht

underwear die Unterwäsche

university die Universität

unleaded bleifrei

until bis

unusual ungewöhnlich

up oben; *up there* da
oben
upward nach oben
urgent dringend
us: it's us wir sind es;
it's for us es ist für
uns; *give it to us*
geben Sie es uns
use der Gebrauch;
(verb) gebrauchen;
it's no use es hat
keinen Zweck
useful hilfreich
usual gewöhnlich
usually gewöhnlich

V

vacancy (room) ein
freies Zimmer
vacation der Urlaub
vaccination die Impfung
vacuum cleaner der
Staubsauger
valley das Tal
valuables die
Wertsachen (f pl)
valve das Ventil
vanilla die Vanille
vase die Vase
veal das Kalbfleisch
vegetable das Gemüse
vegetarian der/die
Vegetarier(in); (adj)
vegetarisch
vehicle das Fahrzeug
very sehr
vest das (Unter)hemd
vet der Tierarzt
video (tape, film) das
Video; *VCR* der
Videorecorder; *video
tape* die Videocassette
Vienna Wien
view der Blick
viewfinder der Sucher
villa die Villa
village das Dorf
vinegar der Essig
violin die Geige
visit der Besuch; (verb)
besuchen
visiting hours die
Besuchszeit
visitor der/die
Besucher(in)
vitamin tablet die
Vitamintablette
vodka der Wodka
voice die Stimme
voicemail die Voice-mail

W

wait warten; *wait!*
warten Sie!
waiter der Ober; *waiter!*
Herr Ober!
waiting room das
Wartezimmer; (station)
der Wartesaal
waitress die Kellnerin;
waitress! Fräulein!
Wales Wales
walk der Spaziergang;
(verb) gehen; *to go for
a walk* spazieren gehen
wall (inside) die Wand;
(outside) die Mauer
wallet die Brieftasche
war der Krieg
wardrobe der
Kleiderschrank
warm warm
was: I was ich war;
he/she/it was
er/sie/es war
wasp die Wespe
watch die (Armband)uhr;
(verb) ansehen
water das Wasser
waterfall der Wasserfall
water heater das
Heißwassergerät
wave die Welle; (verb:
with hand) winken
wavy (hair) wellig
we wir
weather das Wetter
website die Webseite
wedding die Hochzeit
Wednesday Mittwoch
weeds das Unkraut
week die Woche
welcome willkommen;
you're welcome keine
Ursache
well done (steak)
durchgebraten
wellingtons (boots) die
Gummistiefel
Welsh walisisch
Welshman/woman
der/die Waliser(in)
were: you were
(singular informal)
du warst; (singular
formal; plural) Sie
waren; *we/they were*
wir/sie waren
west der Westen
wet naß
what? was?
wheel das Rad
wheelchair der
Rollstuhl; *wheelchair
access* der
Rollstuhlfahrer
when? wann?
where? wo?
whether ob
which? welcher?
whiskey der Whisky
white weiß
who? wer?
why? warum?
wide breit
wife die (Ehe)frau
wind der Wind
window das Fenster;
window box der
Blumenkasten

windshield die
Windschutzscheibe
wine der Wein
wine list die Weinkarte
wing der Flügel
with mit
without ohne
witness der/die Zeuge(in)
woman die Frau
wood (material) das
Holz
wool die Wolle
word das Wort
work die Arbeit; (verb)
arbeiten; (machine,
etc.) funktionieren
worse schlechter
worst schlechtester
wrapping paper das
Packpapier; (for
presents) das
Geschenkpapier
wrench der
Schraubenschlüssel
wrist das Handgelenk
writing paper das
Schreibpapier
wrong falsch

X, Y, Z

X-ray die
Röntgenaufnahme
X-ray department die
Röntgenabteilung
year das Jahr
yellow gelb
yes ja
yesterday gestern
yet: is it ready yet? ist
es schon fertig?; *not
yet* noch nicht
yogurt der Jogurt
you (singular informal)
du; (singular formal;
plural) Sie; *for you* für
dich/Sie; *with you* mit
dir/Ihnen
your (singular
informal) dein;
(singular formal;
plural) Ihr; *your shoes*
deine/Ihre Schuhe
yours: is this yours?
(singular informal)
gehört das dir?;
(singular formal;
plural) gehört das
Ihnen?
youth hostel die
Jugendherberge
ZIP code die Postleitzahl
zipper der
Reißverschluß
zoo der Zoo

Dictionary
German *to English*

The gender of German nouns listed here is indicated by the abbreviations "(m)" for masculine, "(f)" for feminine, and "(nt)" for neuter. Plural nouns are followed by the abbreviations "(m pl)," "(f pl)," and "(nt pl)." The feminine form of most occupations and personal attributes is made by adding -in to the masculine form: **Buchhalter(in)** *accountant*, for example. Exceptions to this rule are listed separately. Where necessary, adjectives are denoted by the abbreviation "(adj)."

A

Abend (m) *evening*
Abendessen (nt) *dinner, supper*
aber *but*
Abfahrt (f) *departure*
Abfall (m) *trash, garbage*
Abfertigungsschalter (m) *check-in* (desk)
Abflug (m) *departures, take-off;* Abflughalle (f) *departure lounge*
Abführmittel (nt) *laxative*
Absatz (m) *heel* (shoe); *sales* (figures)
absichtlich *deliberately*
Abteil (nt) *compartment*
Abteilung (f) *department*
acht *eight*
achtzehn *eighteen*
achtzig *eighty*
Adapter (m) *adapter*
Adresse (f) *address*
Aids *Aids*
Aktentasche (f) *briefcase*
Alkohol (m) *alcohol*
alle(s) *all, every;* alle Straßen *all the streets;* das ist alles *that's all;* alles *everything*
allein *alone*
allergisch *allergic*
alt *old;* wie alt sind Sie? *how old are you?*
am *at, next to;* am Bahnhof *at the station;* am Fenster *next to the window*
Amerika *America*
Amerikaner(in) (m/f) *American* (person)
amerikanisch *American* (adj)
Ampel (f) *traffic lights*
Ananas (f) *pineapple*
andere *another* (different); der/die/das andere ... *the other ...;* ein anderes Zimmer *another room;* das ist

etwas anderes! *that's different!;* etwas anderes *something else;* jemand anders *someone else;* woanders *somewhere else;* ein andermal *another time*
Anfang (m) *start*
anfangen *to start*
Anfänger (m) *beginner*
Angeln (nt) *fishing;* Angeln gehen *to go fishing*
angenehm *nice, pleasant*
anhalten *to stop*
Anhänger (m) *trailer*
ankommen *to arrive*
Ankunft (f) *arrivals*
Anrufbeanworter (m) *answering machine*
anrufen *to call* (phone)
ansehen *to watch*
anstehen *to wait in line*
Antiquitätengeschäft (nt) *antique shop*
Antiseptikum (nt) *antiseptic*
Antragsformular (nt) *application form*
Anzug (m) *suit*
Aperitif (m) *aperitif*
Apfel (m) *apple*
Apotheke (f) *pharmacy*
Appetit (m) *appetite*
Aprikose (f) *apricot*
Arbeit (f) *job, work*
arbeiten *to work*
Arbeitsfläche (f) *countertop*
arm *poor* (not rich)
Arm (m) *arm*
Armband (nt) *bracelet*
Armbanduhr (f) *watch*
Ärmel (m) *sleeve*
Arzt (m) *doctor*
Aschenbecher (m) *ashtray*
Asthma (nt) *asthma*
atmen *to breathe*
attraktiv *attractive*
auch *too* (also)
auf ... *on/at/in ...;* auf der Post *at the post*

office; auf Englisch *in English*
Aufbewahrungslösung (f) *soaking solution* (for contact lenses)
aufgeben *to mail*
aufstehen *to get up* (rise)
Auf Wiedersehen *goodbye*
Auge (nt) *eye;* die Augen *eyes*
Augenarzt/Augenärztin (m/f) *optician*
Augenbraue (nt) *eyebrow*
August *August*
aus *out*
Ausflug (m) *excursion*
Ausgang (m) *exit*
ausgezeichnet *excellent*
Ausländer(in) *foreigner*
Auspuff (m) *exhaust*
ausruhen: sich ausruhen *to rest*
Aussage (f) *statement*
außerhalb *outside*
aussteigen *to get off* (bus, etc.)
Ausstellung (f) *exhibition*
Auster (f) *oyster*
Australien *Australia*
Australier(in) (m/f) *Australian* (person)
australisch *Australian* (adj)
Ausweis (m) *passport*
Auszubildende (m/f) *trainee*
Auto (nt) *car*
Autobahn (f) *expressway*
automatisch *automatic*

B

Baby (nt) *baby*
Bach (m) *stream*
backen *to bake*
Bäcker (m) *baker*
Bäckerei (f) *bakery*
Backofen (m) *oven*
Bad (nt) *bath;* ein Bad nehmen *to take a bath*

Badeanzug (m) *swimsuit*

Badehose (f) *swimming trunks*

Badewanne (f) *bathtub*

Badezimmer (nt) *bathroom*

Bahn (f) *railroad*

Bahnhof (m) *station*

Bahnsteig (m) *platform*

Balkon (m) *balcony*

Ball (m) *ball*

Ballett (nt) *ballet*

Banane (f) *banana*

Band (f) *band* (music)

Bank (f) *bank*

Banknoten (f pl) *(bank)notes*

Bar (f) *bar* (drinks)

Bargeld (nt) *cash*; bar bezahlen *to pay cash*

Bart (m) *beard*

Batterie (f) *battery*

Bauarbeiter(in) *builder*

Bauer (m) *farmer*

Bauernhof (m) *farm*

Baum (m) *tree*

Baumwolle (f) *cotton*

Bayern *Bavaria*

Becken (nt) *basin* (sink)

bedeutet: was bedeutet das? *what does this mean?*

behindert *disabled*

bei Ihnen *at your place*

beide *both*; wir beide *both of us*

beige *beige*

Bein (nt) *leg*; Beinbruch (m) *broken leg*

Beispiel (nt) *example*; zum Beispiel *for example*

beißen *to bite*

Belag (m) *filling* (in sandwich)

Belgien *Belgium*

Belgier(in) (m/f) *Belgian* (person)

belgisch *Belgian* (adj)

Belichtungsmesser (m) *light meter*

Benzin (nt) *gasoline*

Berater(in) *consultant*

Berg (m) *hill, mountain*

Bericht (m) *report*

Berliner (m) *doughnut*

beschäftigt *busy* (occupied)

Bescheinigung (f) *certificate*

besetzt *engaged* (occupied)

Besichtigungen (f) *sightseeing*

besonders *especially*

Besprechung (f) *meeting*

besser *better*

Basteln (nt) *home improvement*

bester *best*

bestreiten *to deny*

Besuch (m) *visit*

besuchen *to visit*

Besucher(in) (m/f) *visitor*

Besuchszeit (f) *visiting hours*

betrunken *drunk*

Bett (nt) *bed*

Bettlaken (nt) *sheet*

Bettwäsche (f) *bed linen*

bewegen *to move*

bezahlen *to pay*

Bezahlung (f) *payment*

BH (m) *bra*

Bibliothek (f) *library*

Bier (nt) *beer*

Bikini (m) *bikini*

Bildschirm (m) *screen, monitor*

billig *cheap*

Biochemie (f) *biochemistry*

bin: ich bin *I am*

Birne (f) *pear*

bis *until*; bis Freitag *by Friday*; bis Morgen *see you tomorrow*; bis bald *see you soon*

Biss (m) *bite* (by dog, etc.)

bißchen *a little*; es ist ein bisschen zu groß *it's a little big*; nur ein bisschen *just a little*

bist: du bist *you are* (informal)

bitte *please*; wie bitte? *pardon?*

bitter *bitter*

Blase (f) *blister*

blass *faint* (unclear), *pale*

Blatt (nt) *leaf*

blau *blue*

blaue Fleck (m) *bruise*

bleichen *to bleach* (hair)

Bleichmittel (nt) *bleach*

bleifrei *unleaded*

Bleistift (m) *pencil*

Bleistiftspitzer (m) *pencil sharpener*

Blick (m) *view*

blind *blind* (cannot see)

Blinker (m) *turn signal*

Blitz (m) *flash* (camera)

blond *blond* (adj)

Blume (f) *flower*

Blumenbeet (nt) *flowerbed*

Blumenkasten (m) *window box*

Blumenkohl (m) *cauliflower*

Blumenladen (m) *florist*

Blumenstecken (nt) *flower-arranging*

Bluse (f) *blouse*

Blut (nt) *blood*

blutig *rare* (steak)

Blutprobe (f) *blood test*

Boden (m) *bottom, floor, ground*; Bodenplane (f) *groundsheet*

Bohnen (n pl) *beans*

Boiler (m) *boiler*

Bonbon (m) *candy*

Boot (nt) *boat* (small)

Bordkarte (f) *boarding pass*

Botschaft (f) *embassy*

Boxen (nt) *boxing*

braten *fry*

Bratpfanne (f) *frying pan*

brauchen *to need*; ich brauche ... *I need ...*

braun *brown*; braun werden *to get a suntan*

braungebrannt *suntanned*

breit *wide*

Breitlauch (nt) *leeks*

Bremse (f) *brake*

bremsen *to brake*

brennen *to burn*

Bridge (nt) *bridge* (game)

Brief (m) *letter* (mail)

Brieffreund(in) (m/f) *penfriend*

Briefkasten (m) *mailbox, letterbox*

Briefmarke (f) *stamp*

Brieftasche (f) *wallet*

Briefträger(in) (m/f) *mail carrier*

Briefumschlag (m) *envelope*

Brille (f) *glasses*

britisch *British*

Brombeere (f) *blackberry*

Brosche (f) *brooch*

Broschüre (f) *brochure, leaflet*

Brot (nt) *bread*

Brötchen (nt) *bread roll*

Brücke (f) *bridge*

Bruder (m) *brother*

Brunnen (m) *fountain*

Brüssel *Brussels*

Brust (f) *chest* (part of body)

Buch (nt) *book*

buchen *to book*

Bücherei (f) *library*

Buchhalter(in) (m/f) *accountant*

Buchhandlung (f) *bookshop*

Buchstabe (m) *letter* (alphabet)

Budget (nt) *budget*

Bügeleisen (nt) *iron* (for clothes)

bügeln *to iron*

Burg (f) *castle*
Bürgersteig (m) *pavement*
Büro (nt) *office*
Bürste (f) *brush*
bürsten *to brush* (hair)
Bus (m) *bus*
Busbahnhof (m) *bus station*
Büstenhalter (m) *bra*
Butter (f) *butter*
Butterbrot (nt) *sandwich*

C

Café (nt) *café*
Campinggas (nt) *camping gas*
Campingplatz (m) *campground*
Campingplatzverwaltung (f) *campground office*
Chips (f) *chips*
Compact-Disc (f) *CD*
Computer (m) *computer*
Computerspiele (nt pl) *computer games*
Couch (f) *sofa*
Creme (f) *cream* (lotion)
Curry (nt) *curry*

D

da *there*
Dach (nt) *roof*
Dachboden (m) *attic*
Dachrinne (f) *gutter*
Dame (f) *lady, woman*
Damenbinden (f pl) *sanitary napkins*
Damentoilette (f) *ladies' room*
Dampfer (m) *steamer* (boat)
Dampfkochtopf (m) *steamer* (cooking)
Däne *Dane* (man)
Dänemark *Denmark*
Dänin *Dane* (woman)
dänisch *Danish*
danken *to thank;* danke *thanks;* danke schön *thank you*
dann *then*
das *the* (nt); das ist Herr ... *this is Mr ...*
Dauerwelle (f) *perm*
Decke (f) *blanket; ceiling*
dein(e) *your* (sing, informal)
Delegierte(r) *delegate*
denken *to think*
Denkmal (nt) *monument*
Deodorant (nt) *deodorant*
der *the* (masculine)
deutsch *German* (adj); Deutsch *German* (language)

Deutsche (m/f) *German* (person)
Deutschland *Germany*
Dezember *December*
Diabetiker(in) *diabetic*
Diamant (m) *diamond* (gem)
dick *fat* (adj: person); *thick*
die *the* (feminine and plural)
Dieb (m) *thief*
Diebstahl (m) *robbery*
Dienstag *Tuesday*
diese: diese Frau *that/this woman*
Diesel (m) *diesel*
dieser: dieser Mann *that/this man*
Dirigent (m) *conductor* (orchestra)
Dokument (nt) *document*
Dollar (m) *dollar*
dolmetschen *to interpret*
Dolmetscher(in) (m/f) *interpreter*
Dom (m) *cathedral*
Donau: die Donau *Danube*
Donnerstag *Thursday*
Doppelzimmer (nt) *double room*
Dorf (nt) *village*
dort drüben *over there*
Dose (f) *can*
Dosenöffner (m) *can opener*
Drahtseilbahn (f) *cable car*
Drehstuhl (m) *swivel chair*
drei *three*
dreihundert *three hundred*
Dreißig *thirty*
dreizehn *thirteen*
dringend *urgent*
dritter *third*
drücken *to push*
Drucker (m) *printer*
du *you* (singular informal)
dumm *stupid*
dunkel *dark*
dünn *thin*
durch *through*
Durchfall (m) *diarrhea*
durchgebraten *well-done* (meat)
Durst (m) *thirst;* ich habe Durst *I'm thirsty*
durstig *thirsty*
Dusche (f) *shower*
Duschgel (nt) *shower gel*

E

Ebbe (f) *low tide*

Ecke (f) *corner*
Ehefrau (f) *wife*
Ehemann (m) *husband*
ehrlich *honest*
Ei (nt) *egg*
Eile: ich bin in Eile *I'm in a hurry*
Eimer (m) *bucket*
Einbrecher (m) *burglar*
einchecken *to check in*
einer von beiden *either of them*
einfach *simple;* einfache Fahrkarte (f) *one-way ticket*
Einfahrt (f) *driveway*
Eingang (m) *entrance*
Einkäufe (f) *shopping* (items bought)
Einkaufen (nt) *shopping* (activity); einkaufen gehen *to go shopping*
Einladung (f) *invitation*
einlösen *to cash*
eins *one* (number); ein Bier/eine Wurst *one beer/one sausage*
Einschreiben (nt) *registered mail*
einsteigen *to get on* (bus, etc.)
Eintrittskarte (f) *admission ticket*
Eintrittspreis (m) *admission charge*
Einwegwindeln (f pl) *disposable diapers*
Einzelzimmer (nt) *single room*
einziger *single* (one)
Eis (nt) *ice, ice cream;* Eiscreme (f) *ice cream;* Eis am Stiel (nt) *ice pop*
Eisen (nt) *iron* (metal)
Eisenwarenhändler (m) *hardware store*
elastisch *elastic*
Elektriker(in) (m/f) *electrician*
elektrisch *electric*
elf *eleven*
Ellbogen (m) *elbow*
Eltern (m pl) *parents*
Empfang (m) *reception*
Empfangsperson (m/f) *receptionist*
Ende (nt) *end*
endlich! *at last!*
eng *narrow, tight*
England *England*
Engländer(in) (m/f) *Englishman(woman)*
englisch *English* (adj); Englisch *English* (language)
Enkel (m) *grandson*
Enkelin (f) *granddaughter*

Entschuldigung! *excuse me!, sorry!*

entweder ... oder ... *either ... or ...*

entwickeln *to develop* (film)

Entzündung (f) *infection*

Epilektiker(in) (m/f) *epileptic*

er *he*

Erbsen (f pl) *peas*

Erdbeeren (f pl) *strawberries*

Erde (f) *soil*

Erdgeschoss (nt) *ground floor*

Erdnüsse (f pl) *peanuts*

Erfrischungen (f pl) *refreshments*

erinnern: sich erinnern *to remember*; ich erinnere mich nicht *I don't remember*

Erkältung (f) *cold* (illness); ich bin erkältet *I have a cold*

Ermäßigungen (f) *discounts*

ernst *serious*

Ersatzteile (nt pl) *spares*

Erste Hilfe (f) *first aid*

erster *first*; erster Klasse *first class*; erste Stock (m) *first floor*

es *it*

Essen (nt) *food, meal*; essen *to eat*

Essig (m) *vinegar*

Etikett (nt) *label*

etwa: etwa 16 *about 16*

etwas *something*

F

Faden (m) *string* (cord)

Fahne (f) *flag*

Fähre (f) *ferry*

fahren *to drive, go* (travel)

Fahrer(in) (m/f) *driver*

Fahrgast (m) *passenger*

Fahrplan (m) *schedule* (train, bus)

Fahrpreis (m) *fare*

Fahrrad (nt) *bicycle*

Fahrstuhl (m) *elevator* (in building)

Fahrt (f) *trip, journey*

Fahrzeug (nt) *vehicle*

fair *fair (just)*

falsch *wrong*

Familie (f) *family*

Fan (m) *fan* (enthusiast)

fantastisch *fantastic*

Farbe (f) *color, paint*

Farbfilm (m) *color film*

fast *almost*

faul *lazy*

Fax (nt) *fax* (document)

faxen *to fax*

Faxgerät (nt) *fax machine*

Februar *February*

Feder (f) *spring* (mechanical)

Fehler (m) *mistake*

Feiertag (m) *public holiday*

Feige (f) *fig*

Feinkostgeschäft (nt) *delicatessen*

Feld (nt) *field*

Fenster (nt) *window*

Fensterladen (m) *shutter*

Ferien (f pl) *holiday*

Fernsehen (nt) *television*; fernsehen *to watch television*

Ferse (f) *heel* (foot)

fertig *ready*; Fertiggerichte (nt pl) *prepared meals*

festmachen *to tie*

Fett (nt) *fat*

feucht *damp*

Feuer (nt) *fire*

Feuerlöscher (m) *fire extinguisher*

Feuerwerk (nt) *fireworks*

Feuerzeug (nt) *lighter*

Feuerzeugbenzin (nt) *lighter fuel*

Fieber (nt) *temperature, fever*

Film (m) *film, movie*

Filter (m) *filter*

Filterpapier (nt) *filter papers*

Finger (m) *finger*

Fisch (m) *fish*

Fischgeschäft (nt) *fishmonger*

flach *flat (level)*

Flasche (f) *bottle*

Flaschenöffner (m) *bottle opener*

Fleisch (nt) *meat*

Fliege (f) *fly* (insect)

fliegen *to fly*

Floh (m) *flea*

Flohspray (nt) *flea spray*

Flöte (f) *flute*

Flug (m) *flight*

Flugnummer (f) *flight number*

Flügel (m) *wing*

Flughafen (m) *airport*

Flughafenbus (m) *airport bus*

Fluglinie (f) *airline*

Flugsteig (m) *gate* (at airport)

Flugzeug (nt) *aircraft*

Fluss (m) *river*

Flut (f) *high tide*

Flyer (m) *leaflet, flyer*

Fön (m) *hair dryer*

Forschungen (f) *research*

Foto (nt) *photograph*

Fotograf (m) *photographer*

fotografieren *to photograph*

Fotokopierer (m) *photocopier*

Frage (f) *question*

Frankreich *France*

Franzose (m) *Frenchman*

Französin (f) *Frenchwoman*

französisch *French*

Frau *Mrs.*

Frau *Ms.*

Frau (f) *woman, wife*

Fräulein *Miss*; Fräulein! *waitress!*

frei *free*

Freitag *Friday*

Fremdenverkehrsbüro (nt) *tourist office*

Freund(in) (m/f) *friend*

freundlich *friendly*

freut mich *pleased to meet you*

Friedhof (m) *cemetery*

Friseur (m) *hairdresser's*

Friseursalon (m) *ladies' hairdresser's*

Fritten (m pl) *french fries*

froh *glad*

Frost (m) *frost*;

Frucht (f) *fruit*; Fruchtsaft (m) *fruit juice*

früh *early*

Frühling (m) *spring* (season)

Frühstück (nt) *breakfast*

fühlen *to feel* (touch)

Führer (m) *guide*

Führerschein (m) *driver's license*

Führung (f) *guided tour*

Füllung (f) *filling* (in tooth, cake)

Fundbüro (nt) *lost property*

fünf *five*

fünfzehn *fifteen*

fünfzig *fifty*

funktionieren *to work* (machine, etc.)

für *for*; für mich *for me*; wofür? *what for?*; für eine Woche *for a week*

furchtbar *awful*

Fuß (m) *foot*; Füße (m pl) *feet*

Fußball (m) *soccer*

Fußboden (m) *floor* (ground)

Fußgänger (m) *pedestrian*; Fußgängerzone (f) *pedestrian zone*

G

Gabel (f) *fork*
Gang (m) *aisle*
ganz *quite* (fully)
Garage (f) *garage* (for parking)
Garantie (f) *guarantee*
garantieren *to guarantee*
Garten (m) *garden*
Gartenarbeit (f) *gardening*
Gartencenter (nt) *garden center*
Gärtner(in) (m/f) *gardener*
Gaspedal (nt) *accelerator*
Gast (m) *guest*
Gastgeber(in) (m/f) *host*
Gasthaus (nt) *inn*
Gebäck (nt) *pastry*
Gebäude (nt) *building*
geben *to give*
Gebiet (nt) *field of work*
Gebiss (m) *dentures, false teeth*
geboren *to be born*: ich bin in ... geboren *I was born in ...*
gebraten *fried*
Gebrauch (m) *use*
gebrauchen *to use*
gebrochen *broken* (arm, etc.)
Geburtstag (m) *birthday*; Herzlichen Glückwunsch! *happy birthday!*
Geburtstagsgeschenk (nt) *birthday present*
Geburtstagskarte (f) *birthday card*
gedämpft *steamed*
gefährlich *dangerous*
Geflügel (nt) *poultry*
Gefrierschrank (m) *freezer*
gegen *against*
gegenüber *opposite*
gegrillt *grilled*
Geheimzahl (f) *PIN (number)*
gehen *to go, walk*; gehen Sie weg! *go away!*
Geige (f) *violin*
Geisteswissenschaften (f pl) *humanities*
Geistliche (m/f) *priest*
gekocht *boiled*
gekochte Schinken (m) *ham*
Gel (nt) *gel* (hair)
gelb *yellow*
Geld (nt) *money*

Geldautomat (m) *ATM*
Geldschein (m) *banknote*
gelegentlich *occasionally*
Gemüse (nt) *vegetable*
Genehmigung (f) *license*
genug *enough*
Gepäck (nt) *luggage*
Gepäckablage (f) *luggage rack*
Gepäckausgabe (f) *baggage claim*
Gepäckschließfach (nt) *left luggage locker*
gerade *just*; es ist gerade angekommen *it's just arrived*
gerecht *fair* (just)
gern: ich schwimme gern *I like swimming*
geröstet *roasted*
Geruch (m) *smell*
Geschäft (nt) *business, shop*
Geschäftsführer (m) *manager*
Geschenk (nt) *gift*; Geschenkpapier (nt) *wrapping paper*
Geschichte (f) *history*
geschieden *divorced*
Geschirrspülmaschine (f) *dishwasher*
Geschirrtuch (nt) *tea towel*
geschlossen *closed*
Geschmack (m) *flavor*
Geschwindigkeit (f) *speed*
Gesicht (nt) *face*
Gespräch (nt) *talk*
gestern *yesterday*
Getränk (nt) *drink*
getrennt *separate(ly)*; wir leben getrennt *we are separated*
Getriebe (nt) *gearbox*
Gewehr (nt) *gun* (rifle)
Gewinn (m) *profits*
Gewitter (nt) *thunderstorm*
gewöhnlich *ordinary, usual, usually*
gibt: es gibt ... *there is/are ...*; gibt es ...? *is/are there ...?*
Gift (nt) *poison*
Gin (m) *gin*
Gitarre (f) *guitar*
Glas (nt) *glass*
gratis *free* (no charge)
glaube: ich glaube ja *I think so*
gleiche: gleiche Kleid *the same dress*
Gleis (nt) *platform*
Glocke (f) *bell* (church)
Glück (nt) *luck*; viel Glück! *good luck!*

glücklich *happy*
Glühbirne (f) *light bulb*
Gold (nt) *gold*
Grafiker(in) (m/f) *designer*
Gras (nt) *grass*
grau *gray*
grell *loud* (color)
Grenze (f) *border*
Grill (m) *barbecue, grill*
groß *big, large, tall*; größer als *bigger than*
Großbritannien *Great Britain*
Großeltern (m pl) *grandparents*
Großmutter (f) *grandmother*
Großstadt (f) *city*
Großvater (m) *grandfather*
grün *green*
Grund (m) *bottom* (sea)
Gruppe (f) *party* (group)
Gummi (m) *rubber* (material)
Gummiband (nt) *elastic band*
Gummistiefel (f) *wellingtons*
Gurke (f) *cucumber*
Gürtel (m) *belt*
gut *good*; mir ist nicht gut *I don't feel well*
gut aussehend *handsome*
Guten Abend *good night*
guten Tag *hello, good day*

H

Haar (nt) *hair*
Haarschnitt (m) *haircut*
Haarspray (nt) *hair spray*
Haarspülung (f) *conditioner*
haben *have*; I have ... ich habe ...; *do you have ...?* haben Sie ...?
Hafen (m) *harbor, port*
Hahn (m) *tap*
Hähnchen (nt) *chicken* (cooked)
halb *half*; eine halbe Stunde *half an hour*
Halbbruder (m) *half-brother*
Halbpension *half-board*
Halbschwester (f) *half-sister*
hallo *hello* (on phone); *hi*
Hals (m) *neck*
Halsband (nt) *collar*
Halskette (f) *necklace*
Halstabletten (f pl) *throat lozenges*
halt! *stop!*
Haltestelle (f) *stop* (bus stop)

Hamburger (m) *hamburger*

Hammer (m) *hammer*

Hamster (m) *hamster*

Hand (f) *hand*

Handbremse (f) *handbrake*

Händedruck (m) *handshake*

Handelsmesse (f) *trade fair*

Handgelenk (nt) *wrist*

Handgepäck (nt) *carry-on luggage*

Handschuhe (f) *gloves*

Handtasche (f) *handbag*

Handtuch (nt) *towel*

Handy (nt) *cell phone*

hart *hard*

hässlich *ugly*

Hauptgericht (nt) *main course*

Hauptstraße (f) *main road*

Haus (nt) *house*; zu Hause *at home*

Haushaltswaren (f pl) *household products*

Hausmeister(in) *caretaker*

Haustiere (nt pl) *pets*

Hautreiniger (m) *skin cleanser*

Hecke (f) *hedge*

Hefter (m) *stapler*

Heftzwecke (f) *thumbtack*

heiß *hot*; mir ist heiß *I feel hot*

heißen *to be called*; wie heißt das? *what's it called?*; wie heißen Sie? *what's your name?*

Heißwassergerät (nt) *water heater*

Heizgerät (nt) *heater*

Heizkörper (m) *radiator*

Heizung (f) *heating*

helfen *to help*

hell *light (not dark)*

Hemd (nt) *shirt*

herauskommen *to get out*

Herd (m) *stove*

hereinkommen *to come in*

Hering (m) *tent peg*

Herr *Mr.*

Herrenfriseur (m) *barber's*

Herrentoilette (f) *men's room*

herunter *down*

Herz (nt) *heart, hearts (cards)*; ich bin herzkrank *I have a heart condition*

herzlichen Glückwunsch! *congratulations!*

Heuschnupfen (m) *hay fever*

heute *today*; heute abend *tonight*

Hilfe (f) *help*

hilfreich *useful*

Himbeeren (f pl) *raspberries*

Himmel (m) *sky*

hinter ... *behind ...*

HIV positiv *HIV-positive*

Hobby (nt) *hobby*

hoch *high*

Hochzeit (f) *wedding*

Hochzeitsreise (f) *honeymoon*

Höhle (f) *cave*

holen *to get (fetch)*

Holland *Holland*

Holländer(in) (m/f) *Dutchman(woman)*

holländisch *Dutch (adj)*

Holz (nt) *wood (material)*

Homöopathie (f) *homeopathy*

Honig (m) *honey*

hören *hear*

Hörgerät (nt) *hearing aid*

Horn (nt) *horn (animal)*

Hose (f) *pants*

Hosenträger (nt pl) *suspenders*

hübsch *nice (attractive)*

Huhn (nt) *chicken (animal)*

Hummer (m) *lobster*

Hund (m) *dog*

hundert *hundred*

Hunger (m) *hunger*; ich habe Hunger *I'm hungry*

Hupe (f) *horn (car)*

husten *to cough*; Husten (m) *cough*

Hut (m) *hat*

I

ich *I*; ich bin *I am*

ihr(e) *their/her*; *your (singular formal)*

im: im Hotel *in the hotel*

Imbiss (m) *snack*

immer *always*

Impfung (f) *vaccination*

in *in*; in der Nacht *at night*

Infektion (f) *infection*

Information (f) *information*

Ingwer (m) *ginger (spice)*

Insekt (nt) *insect*

Insektenmittel (nt) *insect repellent*

Insel (f) *island*

interessant *interesting*

Internet (nt) *internet*

intravenöse Infusion (f) *intravenous drip*

Ire (m) *Irishman*

irgendwie *somehow*

irgendwo *somewhere*

Irin (f) *Irishwoman*

irisch *Irish*

Irland *Ireland*

ist *is*; er/sie/es ist ... *he/she/it is ...*

Italien *Italy*

Italiener(in) (m/f) *Italian*

italienisch *Italian (adj)*

J

ja *yes*

Jacke (f) *jacket*

Jahr (nt) *year*

Jahrmarkt (m) *fair, amusement park*

Jalousie (f) *blinds*

Januar *January*

Jazz (m) *jazz*

Jeans (f) *jeans*

jeder *each, every, everyone*

jemand *somebody*

jetzt *now*

joggen *to jog*; joggen gehen *to go for a jog*

Jogurt (m) *yogurt*

Jucken (nt) *itch*

Jugendherberge (f) *youth hostel*

Juli *July*

Junge (m) *boy*

Juni *June*

Juweliergeschäft (nt) *jeweler*

K

Kabelfernsehen (nt) *cable TV*

Kacheln (f pl) *tiles*

Kaffee (m) *coffee*; Kaffee ohne Milch *black coffee*

Käfig (m) *cage*

Kai (m) *quay*

Kalbfleisch (nt) *veal*

kalt *cold (adj)*; mir ist kalt *I am cold*

Kamera (f) *camera*

Kamm (m) *comb*

Kanada *Canada*

Kanadier(in) (m/f) *Canadian (person)*

kanadisch *Canadian (adj)*

Kanal (m) *canal (m) English Channel*

Kanaltunnel (m) *Channel Tunnel*

Kaninchen (nt) *rabbit*

kann ich ... haben? *can I have ...?*

Kante (f) *side (edge)*

Kanu (nt) *canoe*

kaputt *broken* (machine, etc.)

Karo *diamonds* (cards)

Karotte (f) *carrot*

Karte (f) *card, ticket;* Kartenspiel (nt) *deck of cards*

Kartoffel (f) *potato*

Käse (m) *cheese*

Kasse (f) *box office, checkout*

Kassette (f) *cassette*

Kassettenrecorder (m) *cassette player*

Kassierer(in) *cashier*

Kater (m) *hangover*

Katze (f) *cat*

kaufen *to buy*

Kaufhaus (nt) *department store*

Kaugummi (m) *chewing gum*

Kaution (f) *deposit*

Kehle (f) *throat*

kehren *to sweep*

Keilriemen (m) *fan belt*

kein: ich habe kein Geld *I don't have any money*

keine Ursache *you're welcome*

Keller (m) *cellar*

Kellnerin (f) *waitress*

kennen *to know* (to be acquainted with)

Kerze (f) *candle*

Kilo (nt) *kilo*

Kilometer (m) *kilometer*

Kirmes (f) *fair, amusement park*

Kind (nt) *child*

Kinder *children*

Kinderbett (nt) *crib*

Kindersitz (m) *car seat*

Kinderstation (f) *children's ward*

Kinderwagen (m) *baby carriage*

Kino (nt) *movie theater*

Kirche (f) *church*

Kirsche (f) *cherry*

Kissen (nt) *cushion*

klar *clear*

Klasse (f) *class*

klassische Musik (f) *classical music*

Klavier (nt) *piano*

Kleid (nt) *dress*

Kleider (nt pl) *clothes*

Kleiderbügel *coat hanger (m)*

Kleiderschrank (m) *wardrobe*

klein *little, small*

Kleingeld (nt) *change* (money)

kleinschneiden *to chop, cut*

Klempner(in) (m/f) *plumber*

Klimaanlage (f) *air conditioning*

Klingel (f) *(door) bell*

Klinke (f) *handle* (door)

Klub (m) *club*

klug *clever*

Knie (nt) *knee*

Knoblauch (m) *garlic*

Knöchel (m) *ankle*

Knochen (m) *bone*

Knopf (m) *button*

Koch (m) *cook*

kochen *to boil, cook*

Kochtopf (m) *saucepan*

Köder (m) *bait*

Koffer (m) *suitcase;* Kofferkuli (m) *luggage cart*

Kofferraum (m) *trunk*(car)

Kohl (m) *cabbage*

Kolben (m) *piston*

Köln *Cologne*

komisch *funny*

kommen *to come;* ich komme aus ... *I come from ...;* kommen Sie her! *come here!*

Kommode (f) *chest of drawers*

kompliziert *complicated*

Konditorei (f) *bakery*

Kondom (nt) *condom*

Konferenz (f) *conference*

Konferenzzimmer (nt) *conference room*

Konfitüre (f) *jam*

können Sie ...? *can you ...?*

Konsulat (nt) *consulate*

Kontaktlinsen (f) *contact lenses*

Konzert (nt) *concert*

Kopf (m) *head*

Kopfhörer (m) *headphones*

Kopfkissen (nt) *pillow*

Kopfsalat (m) *lettuce*

Kopfschmerzen (f) *headache*

Kopftuch (nt) *headscarf*

Korb (m) *basket*

Korken (m) *cork*

Korkenzieher (m) *corkscrew*

Körper (m) *body*

Korridor (m) *corridor*

Kosmetika (f) *cosmetics*

kosten *to cost;* was kostet das? *what does it cost?*

kostenlos *free (no charge)*

Kostenvoranschlag (m) *estimate*

Kotelett (nt) *chop (food)*

Krabbe (f) *crab*

Krabben (f pl) *shrimp*

Kragen (m) *collar*

Krampf (m) *cramp*

krank *ill, sick*

Krankenhaus (nt) *hospital*

Krankenpfleger (m) *nurse (man)*

Krankenschwester (f) *nurse (woman)*

Krankenwagen (m) *ambulance*

Krawatte (f) *tie*

Krebs (m) *crayfish*

Kreditkarte (f) *credit card*

Kreuz *clubs (cards)*

Kreuzfahrt (f) *cruise*

Krieg (m) *war*

Krücken (f pl) *crutches*

Küche (f) *kitchen*

Kuchen (m) *cake*

kühl *cool*

Kühler (m) *radiator* (car)

Kühlschrank (m) *refrigerator*

Kunde (m) *client*

Kunst (f) *art*

Kunstgalerie (f) *art gallery*

Künstler(in) (m/f) *artist*

Kupplung (f) *clutch*

Kurort (m) *spa*

kurz *short*

Kusine (f) *cousin (female)*

L

Lächeln (nt) *smile;* lächeln *to smile*

lachen *to laugh*

Lachs (m) *salmon*

Ladegerät (nt) *charger*

Lagerfeuer (nt) *campfire*

Lamm (nt) *lamb (animal)*

Lammfleisch (nt) *lamb (meat)*

Lampe (f) *lamp*

Lampenschirm (m) *lampshade*

Land (nt) *country, land*

landen *to land*

Landkarte (f) *map (of country)*

lang *long*

Länge (f) *length*

langsam *slow*

langweilig *boring*

Laptop (m) *laptop (computer)*

Lastwagen (m) *truck*

laufen *to run*

Läufer (m) *rug (mat)*

laut *loud, noisy*

Leben (nt) *life*

Lebensmittelgeschäft (nt) *grocery store*

Lebensmittelvergiftung (f) *food poisoning*

Leber (f) *liver*

lecker *nice (to eat)*

Leder (nt) *leather*

ledig *single (unmarried)*

leer *empty*

Leerung (f) *pickup (postal)*

legen *to put*

Lehrer(in) *teacher*

Leiche (f) *body* (corpse)

leicht *easy, light* (not heavy)

Leid: es tut mir Leid *I'm sorry*

leihen *to hire*

Leim (m) *glue*

Leine (f) *lead*

Lenkrad (nt) *steering wheel*

lernen *to learn*

Leselampe (f) *reading lamp*

lesen *to read*

letzter *last* (final); *last week* letzte Woche

Leute (m pl) *people*

Licht (nt) *light*

lieb *dear* (person)

Liebe (f) *love*

lieben *to love*; ich mag lieber ... *I prefer ...*

Lied (nt) *song*

Lieferung (f) *delivery*

Liegestuhl (m) *deck chair*

Likör (m) *liqueur*

lila *purple*

Limette (f) *lime* (fruit)

Limonade (f) *lemon soda*

Lineal (nt) *ruler* (for drawing)

links *left* (not right); linke Seite (f) *left side*

Linse (f) *lens*

Lippen-Fettstift (m) *lip salve*

Lippenstift (m) *lipstick*

Liste (f) *list*

Liter (m) *liter*

Locken (f pl) *curls*

Löffel (m) *spoon*

Lounge (f) *lounge* (in hotel)

Luft (f) *air*

Luftmatratze (f) *air mattress*

Luftpost (f) *airmail*

Lutscher (m) *lollipop*

Luxemburg *Luxembourg*

M

machen *to make*; macht nichts *it doesn't matter*

Mädchen (nt) *girl*

Magen (m) *stomach*; Magenschmerzen (f) *stomachache*; Magenverstimmung (f) *indigestion*

Mail (f) *email*; Mail Adresse (f) *email address*

Make-up (nt) *makeup*

Maler(in) *decorator*

Manager(in) *executive*

manchmal *sometimes*

Mandarine (f) *tangerine*

Mann (m) *man, husband*

Manschettenknöpfe (m pl) *cufflinks*

Mantel (m) *coat*

Margarine (f) *margarine*

Markt (m) *market*

Marmelade (f) *jam*

Marmor (m) *marble*

März *March*

Maskara (nt) *mascara*

Matratze (f) *mattress*

Mauer (f) *wall* (outside)

Maus (f) *mouse*

Mechaniker(in) *mechanic*

Medikamente (f) *medication*

Medizin (f) *medicine*

Meer (m) *sea*; Meeresfrüchte (f pl) *seafood, shellfish*

Mehl (nt) *flour*

mehr *more*; Mehrgepäck (nt) *excess baggage*

mehrere *several*

mein(e) *my*

Melone (f) *melon*

Messe (f) *mass* (church)

Messer (nt) *knife*

Metzgerei (f) *butcher's*

mieten *to rent*

Mikrowelle (f) *microwave*

Milch (f) *milk*

Million: eine Million *one million*

Mineralwasser (nt) *mineral water*

Minute (f) *minute*

mir: es gehört mir *it's mine*

mit *with*

Mittag (m) *noon*; Mittagessen (nt) *lunch*

Mitte (f) *center, middle*; in der Mitte *in the middle*

Mitternacht *midnight*

Mittwoch *Wednesday*

Möbel (f) *furniture*

Mobiltelefon (nt) *cell phone*

möchten Sie ...? *would you like ...?*

Mode (f) *fashion*

Modem (nt) *modem*

moderne Architektur (f) *modern architecture*

möglich *possible*; so bald wie möglich *as soon as possible*

Möhre (f) *carrot*

Molkereiprodukte (nt pl) *dairy products*

Monat (m) *month*

Mond (m) *moon*

Monitor (m) *monitor*

Montag *Monday*

Moped (nt) *moped*

Morgen (m) *morning*; am Morgen *in the morning*; morgen *tomorrow*

Motor (m) *engine* (motor)

Motorboot (nt) *motorboat*

Motorhaube (f) *hood* (car)

Motorrad (nt) *motorbike*

müde *tired*

Mülleimer (m) *trashcan*

Mülltonne (f) *garbage can*

Müllsack (m) *garbage bag*

München *Munich*

Mund (m) *mouth*

Münze (f) *coin*

Muschel (f) *shell*

Muscheln (f pl) *mussels*

Museum (nt) *museum*

Musik (f) *music*; Musikanlange (f) *stereo system*; Musikinstrument (nt) *musical instrument*

Musiker(in) *musician*

mussen *to have to (must)*; ich muss ... *I must ...*

Mutter (f) *mother*; *nut* (for bolt)

Mütze (f) *cap* (hat)

N

nach *after, toward*; nach England *to England*

Nachname (m) *last name*

Nachricht (f) *message*

Nachrichten *news*

nächster *next*; nächste Woche *next week*

Nacht (f) *night*

Nachthemd (nt) *nightgown*

Nachtklub (m) *nightclub*

Nachtportier (m) *night porter*

Nachtisch (m) *desserts*

Nachttisch (m) *nightstand*

Nadel (f) *needle*

Nagel (m) *nail* (metal, finger); Nagelfeile (f) *nailfile*; Nagellack (m) *nail polish*

Nagelzwicker (m) *nail clippers*

nah *close, near;* nahe
    der Tür *near the door;*
    in der Nähe von
    London *near London*
nähen *to sew*
Name (m) *name*
Nase (f) *nose*
naß *wet*
Nebel (m) *fog*
neben *beside*
Neffe (m) *nephew*
Negativ (nt) *negative*
    (photo)
nehmen *take*
nein *no* (response)
neu *new*
neun *nine*
neunzehn *nineteen*
neunzig *ninety*
Neuseeland *New
    Zealand*
Neuseeländer(in) (m/f)
    New Zealander
nicht *not;* nicht so viel
    not so much; nicht
    viele *not many*
Nichte (f) *niece*
nichts *nothing*
nie *never*
Niederlande: die
    Niederlande *the
    Netherlands*
niedrig *low*
Niere (f) *kidney*
nirgendwo *nowhere*
noch ein *another one;*
    noch einen Kaffee,
    bitte *another cup of
    coffee, please*
nochmal *again;*
    nochmal dasselbe,
    bitte *same again,
    please*
noch nicht *not yet*
Nockenwelle (f) *camshaft*
Norden (m) *north*
Nordirland *Northern
    Ireland*
Nordsee: die Nordsee
    North Sea
Notausgang (m)
    emergency exit
Notbremse (f)
    emergency brake
Notfall (m) *emergency*
nötig: das ist nicht nötig
    there's no need
Notizblock (m) *notepad*
Notizbuch (nt) *notebook*
notwendig *necessary*
November *November*
Nudeln (f) *pasta*
Nummer (f) *number;*
    Nummernschild (nt)
    license plate
nur *just, only*
Nuss (f) *nut* (fruit)

O

ob *whether*

oben *up;* nach oben
    upward; da oben *up
    there*
Ober (m) *waiter;* Herr
    Ober! *waiter!*
Obst (nt) *fruit*
oder *or*
offen *open* (adj)
öffentlich *public*
öffnen *to open*
Öffnungszeiten *opening
    times*
oft *often*
ohne *without*
ohnmächtig werden *to
    faint*
Ohr (nt) *ear;* Ohren
    (nt pl) *ears*
Ohrringe (m pl) *earrings*
okay *OK*
Oktober *October*
Öl (nt) *oil*
Olive (f) *olive*
Omelette (nt) *omelet*
Onkel (m) *uncle*
Oper (f) *opera*
Operation (f) *operation*
Operationssaal (m)
    operating room
Orange (f) *orange*
    (fruit); orange *orange*
    (color)
Orangenmarmelade (f)
    marmalade
Orangensaft (m) *orange
    juice*
Orchester (nt) *orchestra*
Ort (m) *place* (town,
    etc.)
Osten (m) *east*
Österreich *Austria*
Österreicher(in) (m/f)
    Austrian (person);
    (adj) österreichisch
Ostsee (f) *Baltic Sea*

P

Paar (nt) *pair*
Packpapier (nt)
    wrapping paper
Paket (nt) *package,
    packet, parcel*
Palast (m) *palace*
Panne (f) *breakdown*
    (car)
Pantoffeln (m pl)
    slippers
Papier (nt) *paper*
Paprika (m) *pepper*
    (red/green)
Paraffin (nt) *kerosene*
Parfüm (nt) *perfume*
Park (m) *park*
parken *to park;* Parken
    verboten *no parking*
Parkplatz (m) *parking lot*
Partei (f) *party* (political,
    celebration)
Pass (m) *passport*
Passagier (m) *passenger*

passen Sie auf! *be
    careful!*
Passkontrolle (f)
    passport control
Passwort (nt) *password*
peinlich *embarrassing*
Penizillin (nt) *penicillin*
perfekt *perfect*
Perle (f) *pearl*
Petersilie (f) *parsley*
Pfannkuchen (m)
    pancake
Pfeffer (m) *pepper*
    (spice)
Pfefferminzbonbons (f)
    peppermints
Pfeife (f) *pipe* (for
    smoking)
Pfirsich (m) *peach*
Pflanze (f) *plant*
Pflaster (nt) *adhesive
    bandage*
Pforte (f) *gate* (garden
    gate)
Pfund (nt) *pound*
    (money, weight)
Picknick (nt) *picnic*
Pik *spades* (cards)
Pilot(in) (m/f) *pilot*
Pilz (m) *mushroom*
Pinsel (m) *paint brush*
Pinzette (f) *tweezers*
Pistole (f) *gun* (pistol)
Plastik (nt) *plastic*
Plastiktüte (f) *plastic bag*
Platten (m) *flat tire*
Platz (m) *place, square*
    (in town)
Plätzchen (nt) *cookie*
Pole (m) *Pole* (man)
Polen *Poland*
Polin (f) *Pole* (woman)
Politik (f) *politics*
Polizei (f) *police*
Polizeibericht (m) *police
    report*
Polizeirevier (nt) *police
    station*
Polizist(in) (m/f) *police
    officer*
polnisch *Polish*
Pommes (m pl) *french
    fries*
Popmusik (f) *pop music*
Porrée (m) *leeks*
Portemonnaie (nt) *purse*
Portier (m) *porter*
    (hotel)
Portwein (m) *port*
    (drink)
Porzellan (nt) *china*
Post (f) *mail*
Postamt (nt) *post office*
Poster (nt) *poster*
Postkarte (f) *postcard*
Postleitzahl (f) *ZIP code*
Preis (m) *price*
prima! *great!*
privat *private*
pro *per:* pro Nacht *per
    night*

Problem (nt) *problem*

Professor(in) (m/f) *professor*

prost! *cheers!*

Prothese (f) *dentures, false teeth*

Puder (m) *powder (cosmetics), talcum powder*

Pullover (m) *jumper*

Pulver (nt) *powder*

Pulverkaffee (m) *instant coffee*

Pumpe (f) *pipe (for water)*

Puppe (f) *doll*

Putzfrau (f) *cleaner*

Q, R

Quadrat (nt) *square (shape)*

Qualität (f) *quality*

Qualle (f) *jellyfish*

Quittung (f) *receipt*

Rad (nt) *wheel*

radfahren *to cycle*

Radiergummi (m) *eraser*

Radieschen (nt) *radish*

Radio (nt) *radio*

Rang (m) *circle*

Rasen (m) *lawn*

Rasenmäher (m) *lawnmower*

Rasiercreme (f) *shaving foam*

rasieren: sich rasieren *to shave*

Rasierklingen (f pl) *razor blades*

Rasierwasser (nt) *aftershave*

Rathaus (nt) *town hall*

Ratte (f) *rat*

Rauch (m) *smoke*

rauchen *to smoke*

Raum (m) *room (space)*

Rechen (m) *rake*

Rechner (m) *calculator*

Rechnung (f) *check (bill), invoice*

recht (gut) *fairly (good)*

rechts *right (direction);* rechte Seite (f) *right side*

Rechtsanwalt/Rechtsanwältin (m/f) *lawyer*

reden *to talk*

Regen (m) *rain*

Regenmantel (m) *raincoat*

Regenschirm (m) *umbrella*

Regierung (f) *government*

reich *rich*

reif *ripe*

Reifen (m) *tire*

Reifenpanne (f) *puncture*

Reinigung (f) *dry cleaner*

Reis (m) *rice*

Reise (f) *journey*

Reisebüro (nt) *travel agency*

Reiseführer (m) *guidebook*

Reiseleiter(in) (m/f) *tour guide*

Reisescheck (m) *traveler's check*

Reißnagel (m) *thumbtack*

Reißverschluß (m) *zipper*

Rekord (m) *record (sports, etc.)*

Religion (f) *religion*

Reservierung (f) *reservation*

Rest (m) *rest (remainder)*

Restaurant (nt) *restaurant*

Rettich (m) *radish*

Rezept (nt) *prescription*

Rhabarber (m) *rhubarb*

richtig *right (correct)*

riechen *to smell;* Das riecht gut *that smells good.*

Riegel (m) *bolt (on door)*

Rindfleisch (nt) *beef*

Ring (m) *ring (jewelry)*

Rock (m) *skirt; rock (music)*

Rohr (nt) *pipe (for water)*

Rollstuhl (m) *wheelchair*

Rollstuhlfahrer (m) *wheelchair access*

Rolltreppe (f) *escalator*

Roman (m) *novel*

Röntgenabteilung (f) *X-ray department*

Röntgenaufnahme (f) *X-ray*

rosa *pink*

Rose (f) *rose*

Rosinen (f pl) *raisins*

rot *red*

Rubin (m) *ruby (gem)*

Rücken (m) *back (body)*

Rückfahrkarte (f) *round-trip ticket*

Rücklichter (f pl) *rear lights*

Rucksack (m) *backpack*

Rückseite (f) *back (not front)*

rufen *to shout*

ruhig *quiet*

Ruinen (f pl) *ruins*

Rum (m) *rum*

rund *round (circular)*

Rundreise (f) *tour*

S

sagen *to say;* was haben Sie gesagt? *what did you say?;* wie sagt man ...? *how do you say ...?*

Sahne (f) *cream (for cake, etc.)*

Saite (f) *string (guitar, etc.)*

Salami (f) *salami*

Salat (m) *salad*

Salbe (f) *ointment*

Salz (nt) *salt*

Sammlung (f) *collection (stamps, etc.)*

Samstag *Saturday*

Sand (m) *sand*

Sandalen (f pl) *sandals*

Sandwich (nt) *sandwich*

Satellitenfernsehen (nt) *satellite TV*

satt: ich bin satt *I'm full*

sauber *clean*

Sauna (f) *sauna*

Schach *chess*

Schachtel (f) *box, packet ;* Schachtel Pralinen (f) *box of chocolates*

Schaffner (m) *conductor (bus)*

Schal (m) *scarf*

Schallplatte (f) *record (music)*

Schallplattengeschäft (nt) *record store*

Schalter (m) *switch; ticket kiosk*

Schaltknüppel (m) *gear lever*

Schauer (m) *shower (rain)*

Schaumfestiger (m) *mousse (for hair)*

Scheck (m) *cheque*

Scheckheft (nt) *checkbook*

Scheckkarte (f) *debit card*

Scheinwerfer (m pl) *headlights*

Scheitel (m) *part (hair)*

Schere (f) *scissors*

Schiff (nt) *boat, ship*

Schild (nt) *sign*

Schlaf (m) *sleep*

Schlafanzug (m) *pajamas*

schlafen *to sleep*

Schlaflosigkeit (f) *insomnia*

Schlafsack (m) *sleeping bag*

Schlaftablette (f) *sleeping pill*

Schlafzimmer (nt) *bedroom*

Schlange (f) *line (waiting)*
Schlauch (m) *inner tube*
schlecht *bad, poor (quality)*
schlechter *worse*
schlechtester *worst*
schleudern *to skid*
schließen *to close*
Schlitten (m) *sledge, toboggan*
Schlittschuhe *ice skates*
Schlittschuh laufen gehen *to go ice-skating*
Schloss (nt) *castle*
Schlüssel (m) *key*
Schlussverkauf (m) *sale (at reduced prices)*
Schmerz (m) *ache, pain*
Schmerztablette (f) *painkiller*
Schmuck (m) *jewelry*
schmutzig *dirty*
Schnee (m) *snow*
schneiden *to cut*
schnell *fast, quick*
Schnellimbiss (m) *carry-out*
Schnitt (m) *cut*
Schnuller (m) *pacifier (for baby)*
Schnurrbart (m) *mustache*
Schnürsenkel (m pl) *shoelaces*
Schokolade (f) *chocolate*
schon *already, yet;* ist es schon fertig? *is it ready yet?*
schön *beautiful, pretty*
Schornstein (m) *chimney*
Schotte (m) *Scotsman*
Schottin (f) *Scotswoman*
schottisch *Scottish*
Schottland *Scotland*
Schrank (m) *cupboard*
Schraube (f) *screw*
Schraubenschlüssel (m) *wrench*
Schraubenzieher (m) *screwdriver*
schrecklich *horrible*
Schreibmaschine (f) *typewriter*
Schreibpapier (nt) *writing paper*
Schreiner(in) *carpenter*
Schublade (f) *drawer*
Schuhcreme (f) *shoe polish*
Schuhe (m pl) *shoes*
Schuhgeschäft (nt) *shoe store*
Schule (f) *school*
Schulter (f) *shoulder*
Schüssel (f) *bowl*
schwager *pregnant*

Schwager (m) *brother-in-law*
Schwägerin (f) *sister-in-law*
schwarz *black*
schwarze Johannisbeere (f) *black currant*
Schwarzwald (m) *Black Forest*
Schweinefleisch (nt) *pork*
Schweiß (m) *sweat*
Schweiz: die Schweiz *Switzerland*
Schweizer(in) (m/f) *Swiss (person)*
schweizerisch *Swiss (adj)*
schwer *heavy, hard (difficult)*
Schwester (f) *sister*
schwierig *difficult*
Schwimmbad (nt) *swimming pool*
Schwimmen (nt) *swimming;* schwimmen *to swim*
Schwimmflossen (f pl) *flippers*
schwitzen *to sweat*
schwul *gay (homosexual)*
sechs *six*
sechzehn *sixteen*
sechzig *sixty*
See (m) *lake*
Segelboot (nt) *sailboat*
Segeln (nt) *sailing*
sehen *to see;* ich kann nichts sehen *I can't see*
sehr *very*
Seide (f) *silk*
Seife (f) *soap*
Seil (nt) *rope*
sein(e) *his*
Seite (f) *page, side*
Sekratär(in) (m/f) *secretary*
Sekunde (f) *second (time)*
selbständig *self-employed*
selten *rare (uncommon)*
Seminar (nt) *seminar*
Senf (m) *mustard*
September *September*
Serviette (f) *napkin*
Sessel (m) *armchair*
setzen *put*
Shampoo (nt) *shampoo*
Sherry (m) *sherry*
Shorts (f) *shorts*
sicher *safe, sure;* Sicherheitsgurt (m) *seat belt;* Sicherheitsnadel (f) *safety pin*
Sie *you (singular, formal);* sie *she/they*

sieben *seven*
siebzehn *seventeen*
siebzig *seventy*
Silber (nt) *silver (metal);* silber *silver (color)*
sind: wir/sie/Sie sind; *we/they/you (formal) are*
Singen (nt) *singing;* singen *to sing*
Sirup (m) *syrup*
Sitz (m) *seat*
Skandinavien *Scandinavia*
Skibindung (f) *ski binding*
Skier (m pl) *skis*
Ski fahren *to ski;* Skifahren gehen *to go skiing*
Skilift (m) *ski lift*
Skistiefel (m pl) *ski boots*
Skistöcke (m pl) *ski poles*
Skiurlaubsort (m) *ski resort*
Smaragd (m) *emerald*
so *like this, so*
Socken (f pl) *socks*
Sodawasser (nt) *soda water*
Sofa (nt) *sofa*
sofort *immediately*
Sohn (m) *son*
Sonderangebot (nt) *bargain*
Sonne (f) *sun*
sonnenbaden *to sunbathe*
Sonnenbrand (m) *sunburn*
Sonnenbrille *sunglasses*
Sonnenöl (nt) *suntan lotion*
Sonnenschirm (m) *sunshade*
sonnig *sunny*
Sonntag *Sunday*
sorgfältig *careful*
Soße (f) *sauce*
Souvenir (nt) *souvenir*
sowohl ... als auch ... *both ... and ...*
spät *late*
Spaten (m) *spade (shovel)*
später *later*
spazieren gehen *to go for a walk*
Spaziergang (m) *walk (stroll)*
Speck (m) *bacon*
Speisekarte (f) *menu*
Speiseraum (m) *dining room*
Spiegel (m) *mirror*
Spiel (nt) *match (sport)*
spielen *to play*

Spielzeug (nt) *toy*

Spinat (m) *spinach*

Spinne (f) *spider*

Spitze (f) *lace; tip* (end)

Sport (m) *sport;* Sportzentrum (nt) *gym*

Sportwagen (m) *stroller*

Sprache (f) *language*

Sprachführer (m) *phrasebook*

sprechen *to speak;* sprechen Sie Englisch? *do you speak English?;* ich spreche kein Deutsch *I don't speak German*

Spritze (f) *injection, syringe*

sprudelnd *fizzy (sparkling)*

Sprung (m) *dive*

Sprungbett (nt) *diving board*

Spülmittel (nt) *dishwashing liquid*

stabil *strong, stable* (material)

Stadion (nt) *stadium*

Stadt (f) *town, city*

Stadtplan (m) *town plan, map*

Stadtzentrum (nt) *downtown*

Stadtrand (m) *suburbs*

Stand (m) *stand*

Standlicht (nt) *sidelights*

Star (m) *star* (film)

stark *strong* (person, drink)

Start (m) *start*

Start- und Landebahn (f) *runway*

Station *station* (subway)

Statue (f) *statue*

Stau (m) *traffic jam*

Staubsauger (m) *vacuum cleaner*

Staubtuch (nt) *duster*

Steak (nt) *steak*

stechen *to bite, sting* (insect)

Stecker (m) *plug* (electrical)

Stecknadel (f) *pin*

stehlen *to steal;* es ist gestohlen worden *it's been stolen*

steht: es steht Ihnen *it suits you*

Stein (m) *rock* (stone)

stellen *to put*

Steppdecke (f) *comforter*

sterben *to die*

Stern (m) *star*

Stich (m) *bite, sting* (by insect)

stickig *close* (stuffy)

Stiefel (m) *boot* (footwear)

Stiefmutter (m) *stepmother*

Stiefsohn (m) *stepson*

Stieftochter (m) *stepdaughter*

Stiefvater (m) *stepfather*

Stift (m) *pen*

still *quiet*

stillhalten! *don't move!*

Stimme (f) *voice*

Stock (m) *floor* (story)

Stoff (m) *material* (fabric)

Stöpsel (m) *plug* (sink)

Stoßstange (f) *bumper*

Strand (m) *beach*

Straße (f) *road, street*

Straßenbahn (f) *tram*

Streichholz (nt) *match* (light)

streng *strong* (taste)

stricken *to knit*

Strickwaren (f pl) *knitwear*

Strom (m) *electricity*

Stromanschluss (m) *electrical hookup*

Strümpfe (m pl) *stockings*

Strumpfhose (f) *pantyhose*

Stück (nt) *piece, slice, play* (theatre); fünf Euro das Stück *five euros each*

Student(in) (m/f) *student*

Stuhl (m) *chair*

Stunde (f) *hour, lesson*

Sturm (m) *storm*

Sucher (m) *viewfinder*

Südafrika *South Africa*

Süden (m) *south*

Supermarkt (m) *supermarket*

Suppe (f) *soup*

süß *sweet* (not sour)

Süßigkeit (f) *candy*

Sweatshirt (nt) *sweatshirt*

Synagoge (f) *synagogue*

T

Tabak (m) *tobacco*

Tablett (nt) *tray*

Tablette (f) *pill, tablet*

Tafel Schokolade (f) *bar of chocolate*

Tafelwasser (nt) *still water*

Tag (m) *day*

Tagebuch (nt) *planner*

Tagesdecke (f) *bedspread*

Tagesordnung (f) *agenda*

Tal (nt) *valley*

Tampons (m pl) *tampons*

Tankstelle (f) *gas station*

Tante (f) *aunt*

Tanz (m) *dance*

tanzen *to dance*

Tasche (f) *pocket, bag*

Taschendieb (m) *pickpocket*

Taschenlampe (f) *flashlight*

Taschenmesser (nt) *penknife*

Taschentücher *tissues*

Tasse (f) *cup*

Tastatur (f) *keyboard*

taub *deaf*

tauchen *to dive*

tauschen, umtauschen *to exchange*

tausend *thousand*

Taxi (nt) *taxi*

Taxistand (m) *taxi stand*

Technik (f) *engineering*

Tee (m) *tea;* schwarze Tee *black tea;* Tee mit Milch *tea with milk*

Teilchen (nt) *danish pastry*

Telefon (nt) *telephone*

Telefonbuch (nt) *directory*

telefonieren *to telephone*

Telefonkarte (f) *phone card*

Telefonzelle (f) *telephone booth*

Teller (m) *plate*

Temperatur (f) *temperature*

Tennis (nt) *tennis*

Teppich (m) *carpet*

Termin (m) *appointment*

Terminal (nt) *terminal*

Terrasse (f) *terrace*

Tesafilm (m) *adhesive tape*

teuer *expensive*

Theater (nt) *theater*

tief *deep, low* (voice)

Tiefkühlkost (f) *frozen foods*

Tierarzt (m) *vet*

Tierpass (m) *pet passport*

Tinte (f) *ink*

Tisch (m) *table*

Toast (m) *toast*

Tochter (f) *daughter*

Toilette (f) *toilet*

Toilettenpapier (nt) *toilet paper*

Tomate (f) *tomato*

Tomatensaft (m) *tomato juice*

Tonic (nt) *tonic*

Töpferei (f) *pottery*

Tor (nt) *gate*
tot *dead*
Tourist(in) *tourist*
Tradition (f) *tradition*
Tragetasche (f) *plastic bag*
Trainingsanzug (m) *jogging suit*
Traktor (m) *tractor*
trampen *to hitchhike*
Trauben (f pl) *grapes*
traurig *sad*
Treffen (nt) *meeting*
Treppe (f) *stairs, staircase*
trinken *to drink*
Trinkgeld (nt) *tip (money)*
Trinkwasser (nt) *drinking water*
trocken *dry*
Tropfen (f) *drops*
Truhe (f) *chest (furniture)*
tun *to do*
Tunnel (m) *tunnel*
Tür (f) *door*
Türke *Turk* (man)
Türkin *Turk* (woman)
Türkei: die Türkei *Turkey*
türkisch *Turkish*
Turm (m) *tower*
Turnschuhe *athletic shoes*

U

U-Bahn (f) *subway, metro*
U-Bahnstation (f) *subway station*
übel: mir ist übel *I feel sick*
über *over, across, more than*
überall *everywhere*
Überführung (f) *overpass*
überfüllt *crowded*
übergeben: sich übergeben *to be sick (vomit)*
überholen *to overtake*
Überlandbus (m) *bus (long-distance)*
übersetzen *to translate*
Übersetzer(in) (m/f) *translator*
Überzelt (nt) *fly sheet*
Uhr (f) *clock, watch*
um 3 Uhr *at 3 o'clock*
Umhängetuch (nt) *shawl*
umziehen *to move (house)*
umziehen: sich umziehen *to change (clothes)*
und *and*
Unfall (m) *accident*

Unfallstation (f) *emergency room*
ungewöhnlich *unusual*
Universität (f) *university*
Unkraut (nt) *weeds*
unmöglich *impossible*
unten *down;* hier unten *down here*
unter ... *below ..., under ...*
Untergeschoss (nt) *basement*
Unterhaltung (f) *entertainment*
Unterhemd (nt) *vest*
Unterhose (f) *underpants*
Unterkunft (f) *accommodation*
Unterrock (m) *underskirt*
Untertasse (f) *saucer*
Unterwäsche (f) *underwear*
Urlaub (m) *vacation*

V

Vanille (f) *vanilla*
Vase (f) *vase*
Vater (m) *father*
Vegetarier(in) (m/f) *vegetarian* (person)
vegetarisch *vegetarian* (adj)
Verkehrsbüro (nt) *tourist office*
Ventil (nt) *valve*
Ventilator (m) *fan (ventilator)*
Verband (m) *bandage*
Verbrennung (f) *burn*
Vergaser (m) *carburetor*
vergessen *to forget*
Vergrößerung (f) *enlargement*
verheiratet *married*
Verhütungsmittel (nt) *contraceptive*
verkaufen *to sell*
Verkäufer(in) (m/f) *shopkeeper*
Verkehr (m) *traffic*
Verlängerungsschnur (f) *extension cord*
Verletzung (f) *injury*
verlobt *engaged (couple)*
Verlobte (m/f) *fiancé(e)*
Vermittlung (f) *operator*
verriegeln *to bolt*
verrückt *mad*
verschieden *different*
Verschluss (m) *cap (bottle), shutter (camera)*
Versicherung (f) *insurance*
verspätet *delayed*
Verspätung: der Bus hat

Verspätung *the bus is late*
verstehen *understand;* ich verstehe *I see/I understand;* ich verstehe nicht *I don't understand*
versuchen *to try*
Vertrag (m) *contract*
Vertreter (m) *agent*
Verwandte (m) *relative*
Verzeihung! *sorry! (apology)*
Vetter (m) *cousin (male)*
Video (nt) *video*
Videocassette *video tape* (f)
Videorecorder (m) *video recorder*
viel *a lot, much*
vielleicht *maybe, perhaps*
vier *four*
Viertel (nt) *quarter*
vierter *fourth*
vierzehn *fourteen*
vierzig *forty*
Villa (f) *villa*
Visitenkarte (f) *business card*
Vitamintablette (f) *vitamin tablet*
Vogel (m) *bird*
Voice-mail (f) *voicemail*
Volksmusik (f) *folk music*
voll *busy (bar, etc.), full*
Vollpension *full board*
von *of*
vor ... *before ..., in front of ...*
vorbei *over (finished)*
Vorgesetzte (m/f) *superior*
Vorhang (m) *curtain*
Vorhängeschloss (nt) *padlock*
Vorlesungssaal (m) *lecture hall*
Vorname (m) *first name*
Vorspeisen (f pl) *appetizers*
Vortrag (m) *presentation*

W

Wächter (m) *guard*
Wagen (m) *car (train)*
wahr *true*
während *during*
Wald (m) *forest*
Wales *Wales*
Waliser(in) (m) *Welshman/ Welshwomam*
walisisch *Welsh*
Wand (f) *wall (inside)*
Wandern (nt) *hiking*

Wandteppich (m) *tapestry*

wann? *when?*

war *was*; ich war *I was*; er/sie/es war *he/she/it was*

waren *were*; wir/sie waren *we/they were*; Sie waren *you (formal) were*

warm *warm*

warst *were*; du warst *you* (informal) *were*

warten *wait*; warten Sie! *wait!*

Wartesaal (m) *waiting room* (station)

Wartezimmer (nt) *waiting room*

warum? *why?*

was? *what?*; was ist das? *what's that/this?*

Waschbecken (nt) *bathroom sink*

Wäsche (f) *laundry* (dirty clothes)

Wäscheklammer (f) *clothespin*

Wäscherei (f) *laundry* (place)

Waschpulver (nt) *laundry detergent*

Waschsalon (m) *laundromat*

Wasser (nt) *water*; Wasser mit Kohlensäure, das Sprudelwasser *sparkling water*; Wasser ohne Kohlensäure *still water*

Wasserfall (m) *waterfall*

Wasserkessel (m) *teakettle*

Watte (f) *cotton balls*

Webseite (f) *website*

Wechselkurs (m) *exchange rate*

wechseln *to change* (money)

Wecker (m) *alarm clock*

weder ... noch ... *neither ... nor ...*

Weg (m) *path*

weich *soft*

Weihnachten (nt) *Christmas*

weil *because*

Wein (m) *wine*; Weinkarte (f) *wine list*

Weinbrand (m) *brandy*

weinen *to cry* (weep)

weiß *white*

weit *far*; wie weit ist es? *how far is it?*; ist es weit von hier? *is it far away?*

welcher? *which?*

Welle (f) *wave*

wellig *wavy* (hair)

weniger *less*

wenn *if*

wer? *who?*

Werkstatt (f) *car repairs, garage*

Wertsachen (f pl) *valuables*

Wespe (f) *wasp*

Westen (m) *west*

Wetter (nt) *weather*

Whisky (m) *whisky*

wie? *how?*; wie heißen Sie? *what's your name?*; wie spät ist es? *what time is it?*

Wien *Vienna*

willkommen *welcome*

Wimperntusche (f) *mascara*

Wind (m) *wind*

Windel (f) *diaper*

Windschutzscheibe (f) *windshield*

winken *to wave*

wir *we*

wissen *to know* (a fact); ich weiß nicht *I don't know*

Witz (m) *joke*

wo? *where?*

Woche (f) *week*

Wodka (m) *vodka*

Wohnmobil (nt) *camper van*

Wohnung (f) *apartment, flat*

Wohnwagen (m) *caravan*

Wohnzimmer (nt) *lounge* (in house)

Wolldecke (f) *rug* (blanket)

Wolle (f) *wool*

Wort (nt) *word*

Wörterbuch (nt) *dictionary*

Wurst (f) *sausage*

Z

Zahl (f) *number*

Zahn (m) *tooth*

Zahnarzt (m) *dentist*

Zahnbürste (f) *toothbrush*

Zahnpasta (f) *toothpaste*

Zahnschmerzen (f) *toothache*

Zäpfchen (nt) *suppository*

Zaun (m) *fence*

zehn *ten*

zehntausend *ten thousand*

Zeit (f) *time*

Zeitplan (m) *schedule*

Zeitschrift (f) *magazine*

Zeitung (f) *newspaper*

Zeitungsladen (m) *newsstand*

Zelt (nt) *tent*

Zeltboden (m) *groundsheet*

Zeltstange (f) *tent pole*

Zentrale (f) *headquarters*

Zentralheizung (f) *central heating*

zerbrochen *broken* (vase, etc.)

Zeuge(in) (m/f) *witness*

ziehen *pull*

ziemlich *fairly, quite*

Zigarette (f) *cigarette*

Zigarre (f) *cigar*

Zimmer (nt) *room*

Zimmermädchen (nt) *maid*

Zimmerservice (m) *room service*

Zitrone (f) *lemon*

Zoll (m) *Customs*

zollfrei *duty-free*

Zoo (m) *zoo*

zu *too* (excessively)

Zucker (m) *sugar*

Zug (m) *train*

zum *to*; zum Bahnhof *to the station*

Zündkerze (f) *spark plug*

Zündung (f) *ignition*

Zunge (f) *tongue*

zurückgeben *to return* (give back)

zurückkommen *to return* (come back)

zusammen *together*

Zusammenbruch (m); *nervous breakdown*

Zuschlag (m) *supplement*

zwanzig *twenty*

Zweck(m) *purpose*; es hat keinen Zweck *it's no use*

zwei *two*; zwei Einzelbetten *twin beds*; zwei Wochen *two weeks*

Zweigstelle (f) *branch*

zweiter *second* (in series); zweiter Klasse *second class*

Zwiebel (f) *onion*

zwischen ... *between ...*

zwölf *twelve*

Acknowledgments

The publisher would like to thank the following for their help in the preparation of this book: Edith and Dieter Gollnow for the organization of location photography in Germany; Die Bahn DB, Deutsche Bahn AG, Hannover; Üstra Hannoversche Verkehrsbetriebe AG, Hannover; Raustaurant: Der Gartensaal im Neuen Rathaus, Hannover; Sprengel-Museum Hannover; Polizei-Direktion Hannover; Café An der Martkirche, Hannover; Teestübchen Am Ballhof; Europa-Apotheke, Hannover; Wochenmarkt Gretchenstraße; Magnet Showroom, Enfield; MyHotel, London; Kathy Gammon; Juliette Meeus and Harry.

Language content for Dorling Kindersley by G-AND-W PUBLISHING
Managed by **Jane Wightwick**
Editing and additional input: **Sam Fletcher, Christopher Wightwick**

Additional design assistance: **Lee Riches, Fehmi Cömert, Sally Geeve**
Additional editorial assistance: **Paul Docherty, Mary Lindsay, Lynn Bresler**
Picture research: **Louise Thomas**

Picture credits

Key:
t=top; b=bottom; l=left; r=right; c=center; A=above; B=below

p2 Alamy RF: Chris Warham; **p4/5** Alamy RF: Goodshoot tr; **p6/7** Laura Knox: cl; **p10/11** Alamy RF: BananaStock cAr, bl; RubberBall cBl; **p12/13** Alamy RF: John Foxx cAr; RubberBall br; DK Images: cl; Steve Shott cBr; Ingram Image Library: tr, cr; **p14/15** Alamy RF: Comstock Images tcr; Ingram Image Library: cAl, cl, cBl, cAr, cBr, bcr; **p16/17** Alamy RF: RubberBall bcr; Ingram Image Library: tr; **p18/19** Alamy: Foodfolio cr; DK Images: David Murray tr; Ian O'Leary clB; **p22/23** Alamy RF: Image Source crA; Think Stock br; DK Images: cl; Susanna Price br; Magnus Rew tcrB; Ingram Image Library: tcr; **p24/25** Alamy: Archivberlin Fotoagentur GmbH clA, Dave King tcr; **p26/27** Ingram Image Library: cl; **p28/29** DK Images: Dave King cr; Stephen Oliver tcr; Matthew Ward bclA; Ingram Image Library: bcrA, bcr; **p30/31** Alamy RF: Comstock Images bcl; DK Images: cl, bclA; Andy Crawford crA; **p34/35** Ingram Image Library: tcr; **p36/37** DK Images: bcl, bcr; Magnus Rew cl; Ingram Image Library: bl; **p38/39** Alamy RF: Imageshop / Zefa Visual Media cl; **p40/41** Alamy: Archiv Fotoagentur GmbH bcr; DK Images: Dorota and Mariusz Jarymowicz cl; **p42/43** Alamy: Michael Klinec tcrB; Alamy RF: Comstock Images cAr; Goodshoot br; Nigel Schermuly: cr; **p44/45** Courtesy of Audi UK c; **p46/47** Alamy RF: Imageshop / Zefa Visual Media br; Courtesy of Audi UK: tcr; DK Images: Dorota and Mariusz Jarymowicz bcl, br; Ingram Image Library: tclB; Nigel Schermuly: cr; **p48/49** Alamy RF: Chris Warham c; DK Images: Dorota and Mariusz Jarymowicz bcl; **p50/51** Alamy: Andre Jenny c; **p52/53** Alamy: Pat Behnke tcrB; Alamy RF: Image Farm Inc cAr; DK Images: cl; **p54/55** Alamy: Jackson Smith bclA; Alamy RF: BananaStock cl; John Foxx c; Image Source cAr; ThinkStock tcr; DK Images: Andy Crawford bcl; **p56/57** Alamy RF: Goodshoot clA; Chris Warham cl; Courtesy of Audi UK: bc; DK Images: Dorota and Mariusz Jarymowicz tl, clAA; **p58/59** Alamy: Michael Juno tcr; Alamy RF: Brand X Pictures cBl, cBBl; Image Source cAAl; DK Images: cAl; **p60/61** Alamy: Robert Harding Picture Library bcr; Alamy RF: imagebroker bl; Image Source cAr; DK Images: Steve Gorton tcrB; Pia Tryde cAAr; Ingram Image Library: tcr; **p62/63** DK Images: Stephen Whitehorn c; **p64/65** Alamy: Arcaid bcrA; Dennis Hallinan c; Alamy RF: GKPhotography cBr; Goodshoot cAAr; Justin Kase tcrB; DK Images: Steve Tanner cAr; Ingram Image Library: tcr; **p66/67** Alamy: Arcaid tl; Alamy RF: Image Source cAr; DK Images: tr; Stephen Whitehorn bl; Ingram Image Library: br; **p68/69** Alamy: Balearic Pictures cr; Alamy RF: Celestial Panoramas cAl; **p70/71** Ingram Image Library: cr; **p72/73** Alamy RF: imagebroker tcrB; Image Source cAr; Comstock Images tcr; Elizabeth Whiting & Associates bl; **p74/75** Alamy RF: Doug Norman bl; Ingram Image Library: cr; **p76/77** Alamy: Balearic Pictures cBl; Alamy RF: Celestial Panoramas Ltd bcl; **p80/81** Getty: Taxi / Rob Melnychuk bc; Ingram Image Library: cAr; Xerox UK Ltd: tcr; **p82/83** Alamy: wildphotos.com tcr; Alamy RF: FogStock cAAl; Momentum Creative Group cAl; Shoosh / Up the Res cBl; Ingram Image Library: cl; **p84/85** Alamy: Brand X Pictures cr; fl Online c; Alamy RF: image100 tc; SuperStock tcr; Ingram Image Library: crB; **p86/87** Getty: Taxi / Rob Melnychuk tc; **p90/91** Alamy RF: Brand X Pictures tcr; DK Images: cl; David Jordan cr; Stephen Oliver cr; Ingram Image Library: cBr; **p92/93** Alamy RF: Pixland cr; DK Images: cl; Guy Ryecart tr; **p94/95** Alamy: David Kamm cl; Phototake Inc bcl; Alamy RF: Comstock Images cr; ImageState Royalty Free bcr; DK Images: Stephen Oliver br; **p96/97** Alamy RF: Pixland br; DK Images: tl; Ingram Image Library: tr; **p98/99** Alamy: Bildarchiv Monheim GmbH / Jochen Helle c; Alamy RF: ThinkStock br; DK Images: Jake Fitzjones bl; Peter Kindersley cr; **p100/101** Alamy: Steve Gorton tcr; **p102/103** Alamy: The Garden Picture Library tcr cAAl; Alamy: Hortus b; D Hurst tcrB; Ingram Image Library: cAr; **p104/105** DK Images: Paul Bricknell cl(6); Jane Burton bcl; Geoff Dann cl(2); Max Gibbs cl(4); Frank Greenaway cl(3); Dave King cl(1), cAr; Tracy Morgan c(5); **p106/107** Alamy: The Garden Picture Library br; DK Images: Peter Kindersley cr; **p108/109** Alamy RF: John Foxx tc; **p110/111** Alamy RF: RubberBall cr; DK Images: Andy Crawford cl; **p112/113** Alamy RF: Image Source cl; DK Images: Dave King bcl; Steve Shott bl; Ingram Image Library: bcrA; **p114/115** Alamy RF: FogStock tcr; Alamy RF: Image Source cAr; Index Stock cAl; **p116/117** Alamy: The Garden Picture Library cAl; Alamy RF: clB; **p118/119** DK Images: Steve Gorton cr; **p120/121** Alamy: ImageState / Pictor International cl; Shotfile cBl; Alamy RF: Sarkis Images tcr; DK Images: bcl; **p122/123** Alamy RF: BananaStock br; Ingram Image Library: cAr; Alamy: ImageState / Pictor International bclA; Shotfile cBl; DK Images: bcl; Paul Bricknell tc(5); Geoff Dann tc(3); Max Gibbs tc(1); Frank Greenaway tc(2); Dave King tc(4); Tracy Morgan tc(6); Ingram Image Library: bl; **p126/127** Alamy RF: Pat Behnke blA; Alamy RF: Image Farm Inc bcl; **p128** DK Images.

All other images **Mike Good**.